GO ASK YOUR

Father

Also by Lennard J. Davis

MY SENSE OF SILENCE: MEMOIRS OF A
CHILDHOOD WITH DEAFNESS

THE SONNETS: A NOVEL

SHALL I SAY A KISS? THE COURTSHIP LETTERS
OF A DEAF COUPLE, 1936–1938

OBSESSION: A HISTORY

GO ASK YOUR

Father

One Man's Obsession with Finding His

Origins Through DNA Testing

Lennard J. Davis

BANTAM BOOKS

GO ASK YOUR FATHER
A Bantam Book / June 2009

Published by Bantam Dell
A Division of Random House, Inc.
New York, New York

Book design by Ellen Cipriano

Bantam Books and the Rooster colophon are registered trademarks of
Random House, Inc.

Library of Congress Cataloging-in-Publication Data
Davis, Lennard J., 1949–
Go ask your father : one man's obsession with finding his origins through
DNA testing / Lennard J. Davis.
p.   cm.
ISBN 978-0-553-80551-2 (hardcover)
1. Davis, Lennard J., 1949– 2. Artificial insemination, Human—Biography.
3. DNA fingerprinting—Popular works. I. Title.

HQ761.D38 2009
306.87092—dc22
[B]
2008042599

Printed in the United States of America
Published simultaneously in Canada

www.bantamdell.com

BVG   10 9 8 7 6 5 4 3 2 1

To my wife, whose love helps me
understand truly who I am

CONTENTS

CONTENTS

GO ASK YOUR

Father

*There was a man dining with us one day who had had
far too much wine and shouted at me—half-drunk and shouting
that I was not rightly called my father's son.*

—SOPHOCLES,
OEDIPUS TYRANNUS

Prologue: Little Oedipus

IT IS A GRIM SATURDAY MORNING IN the Bronx in 1957. The wind whistles outside the windows of a dingy synagogue as I peer through the smudged stained-glass window of the small room adjacent to the main hall. I've chosen to see the world through the cobalt-blue pane, my favorite hue. Amethyst trees strain against the force of the royal blue wind while indigo birds wheel in the sky. Inside the *shul*, the men are chanting in their lugubrious voices the Hebrew prayers, which undulate in minor keys, praising the power of Yahweh. The women, behind a curtain on the side of the room, sing their plaintive counterpoint.

Those of us with living parents have been called into the small anteroom so that those with dead parents can recite the *kiddush*, the prayer for the departed, in unison. The recently bereaved and those celebrating the anniversary of the death intone: *"Yeetgadal v' yeetkadash sh'mey rabbah,"* followed by the Eastern European *"Ormain!"* for "Amen." Nothing sounds sadder than that prayer. I don't question the wisdom of this tradition, but I am thankful that my mother and father are alive and padding around our one-bedroom apartment a few blocks away. I've come on Saturday morning all by myself to attend the Sabbath services. I've just turned eight and am feeling quite worldly in my independence, and very religious, sanctified, and holy. During the reading of the Torah, we young ones will be taken upstairs to the even dingier Dickensian halls of the Talmud Torah school, where we will be told Bible stories, allowed to play games such as Steal the Kosher Bacon, and be given at last the Nestlé's chocolate bars that I love and crave—probably the ultimate reason I like going to Sabbath services.

Suddenly, a boy claps his hand on my shoulder. He is a year or two older. There is a strangely demented look in his eyes. For no apparent reason, except for the joy of spreading information or perhaps of trumping a younger boy with astounding news, he quizzes sotto voce: "Hey, know what your parents did to get you born?"

"Sure," I say, not really knowing.

"What?"

"I . . . I . . ."

He doesn't wait. He can't wait, really.

"Your father put his dick in your mother."

This is a little confusing since he doesn't seem to have completed the sentence. Into my mother? I know what a dick is, and the idea that my father put his dick into my mother is instantly unappealing. I had used my dick for something called "pee-pee," and not much else. The idea of me, for example, putting my dick in Jill Schwartz, my upstairs neighbor, seemed not only rude but also unpleasant. And where would I put it into her? That raised other unseemly questions.

So I respond categorically, "My father did not put his dick into my mother." My father was British and so was my mother. They were very proper and never even used *dick*. They used *wee-wee* to me and *penis* when they had to, both of which were the more polite words said by the better sort of people. I was sure that if the president ever said anything about his dick, in the privacy of his own home, to his mother, he would have used *wee-wee*, as I did.

But the boy insists, now with glee. I can hear the old men and women chanting for their dead parents. Did those revered and departed men and women condone the fact that Jewish men's dicks, rabbis' dicks, were put into Jewish women, rabbis' wives? I strongly doubt it. Jewish history and culture seemed opposed to that idea. For one thing, it wouldn't have been kosher, I feel sure.

I say with a clear finality, "My father never put his dick into my mother to have me."

The boy laughs. "You'll see. You'll learn."

I don't want to believe this. The boy is wrong. The azure wind blowing through the amethyst trees knows that he is wrong. The world glimpsed through my cobalt-colored stained glass knows he is wrong. My teachers at public school would back me up.

As the prayer for the dead ends, we are ushered back into the main hall. The deceased have been mourned; parenthood has been uplifted; all is well. Now it is time to sing more prayers in anticipation of the chocolate bar awaiting us upstairs.

But that problem—did my father put his dick into my mother

to have me?—would, strangely enough, resurface many years later, not in the way the boy meant but in a much more profound way. Eventually I did of course learn about sex, about the birds and the bees, but, like Oedipus, I still had much more to learn about myself and the truth of my origins.

ONE

A Phone Call and Its Consequences

IT WAS JUNE 2, 1981, and I was in my apartment on Morningside Drive in New York City working on a new book. A professor in the Columbia University Department of English, married, with a one-year-old son, I had a life that seemed pretty steady. At that particular moment, however, I was grieving. My father, Morris Davis, had died a week earlier, just before his eighty-third birthday, after a long, slow decline caused by prostate cancer.

Born in 1949, I was the son of Morris and Eva, and I had grown up in the Bronx with my brother, Gerald. Aside from the fact that my parents were both deaf and we spoke sign language at home, ours was a typical, ordinary family. I felt sure that I understood the basic contours of my life as well as anyone else did.

But this was a difficult time. I was still feeling the strangeness of being an orphan. My mother had died ten years before, having been hit by a truck while crossing the street when I was twenty-two years old. And now my father, too, was dead, a mere two days after slipping into a coma.

The phone rang, taking me away from my work. It was a call from my uncle Abie, my father's younger brother. We began talking about dividing up some of my father's possessions. As we were discussing these details, I remembered that a month or two earlier Abie had taken me aside at my father's hospital bed and said in an unwelcome, confidential tone, "I've got a secret, but I can't say what it is until your father dies."

At the time I had shrugged off Abie's sepulchral whisper in my ear as yet another of the odd and annoying things that had come out of his mouth over the years. Abie was someone my father and mother had held in low esteem. Whenever they talked about him, they presented him as an example of what not to be like: he was always late and always impulsive, and he did things that I was told not to do. These were rather ordinary things that, I learned later in life, many people did—things such as read in bed, read on the toilet, and hang around the house in his pajamas all morning. But there was a particular urgency in the way I was encouraged not to do such things. My father, Morris, was a precise, orderly man of British birth who prided himself on punctuality and control. He was a man who went to sleep when his head hit the pillow, emptied his bowels on schedule and without the aid of printed matter, arrived on time, and got up in the morning dressed for action. Abie was his opposite, his less superego-driven counterpart. In addition, having lost one wife when he was younger and divorced another in later years, Abie had dated a constantly changing stream of women even into his seventies—in sharp contrast to my father's lifelong history of steady and devoted monogamy. In our family, Abie was what one should not be. Not exactly a rebel, but someone without a cause.

Now, as I talked to Abie on the telephone, I suddenly remembered his knowing whisper at my father's deathbed.

"By the way, what was that secret you said you'd tell me after my father died?" I asked.

"Oh, nothing. Forget about it." Abie still had traces of a British accent that my father never had because Morris became deaf before he could speak.

"Come on! You said there was a secret. Since you mentioned it, you really have to tell me."

"No, it's not important."

He demurred; I insisted.

Finally he took a breath and said: "You know, there are ten years between you and your brother, and that was because your parents had trouble having another child. Well, when they finally realized they couldn't, they asked me for help."

I didn't get it. Then he added, "Well, I don't know how to say this, but I am your father."

There was a long pause. The last four words hung in the air like a sword of Damocles. My father's body was barely settled in its grave; my grief was still fresh.

"You..." I trailed off.

"It's not what you think."

I had immediately conjured up the distasteful image of my uncle and my mother locked in a forbidden embrace. That thought, given all I knew of my uncle, wasn't impossible, but from what I knew of my mother, it appeared highly unlikely.

"It was..." He hesitated for the words. "What do you call it? Artificial insemination."

This story was sounding fishier every minute. Did they even have artificial insemination in January 1949, the month and year I was conceived?

"Your father came to my store on Fourteenth Street, where I was making leather novelties, and he had a jar."

"A jar? What kind of a jar?"

"I don't remember. Just a jar, a tube. He asked me to, you know, put some semen in it. I went to the men's room and did."

I had an even more distasteful image of my uncle masturbating in the smelly bathroom of his grimy workshop.

"Nine months later you were born." Abie said this in his high, nasal, lower-class British accent, which had become somewhat Americanized. It was an unpleasant voice, metallic, whiny, and in-sinuating. So was that how I was conceived? No candles or flowers, no romance, no glint in the eye—just a quick jerk-off in a rank toilet?

I couldn't say anything. The whole idea seemed so far-fetched and impossible. My parents had repeatedly told me how they "tried" to have me. How long it took. How difficult it was. It always struck me as an embarrassing but also funny tale. How hard could it have been to "try"? Sex is fun and enjoyable, isn't it? Why had they looked so tormented when they told that story? After all, I was born. Here I was. I had always imagined some vast and chronic in-vestment of sexual energy that ultimately produced me. And even though they had told me of the difficulty, the story always had a happy ending, with my triumphant birth and their collective bliss and tears of joy. My brother had always told me how pleased he was, at ten years old, to have a little brother. It was a family romance culminating in happiness and success. Wasn't it?

If Abie's story was true, why had they never spoken or signed a word to me about this strangely dark tale that was now unfolding?

Abie continued in an insinuating tone that was becoming more and more disconcerting to me: "You know, you are very bright. I always followed your achievements. Your father was, you know, intelligent, but he was deaf. How well you did at school, I always knew that was because of me. I was proud of you. When you got into Columbia University, got your Ph.D., I knew that was because I was your father. Now you are a professor at Columbia. I'm proud of that." Was he insulting my father, who had just died? Was Abie crowing over his sexual and intellectual superiority to his deaf brother?

The whole thing seemed so ludicrous and so much like the nineteenth-century novels I wrote about in my work as an English professor that I began to feel like a character in an elaborate plot. There was a scene in a George Eliot novel, *Felix Holt*, that came instantly to mind. Harold Transome's argument with an older man named Jermyn, who is his enemy, is becoming more physical and violent.

By this time every body's attention had been called to this end of the room, but both Jermyn and Harold were beyond being arrested by any consciousness of spectators.

"Let me go, you scoundrel!" said Harold, fiercely, "or I'll be the death of you."

"Do," said Jermyn, in a grating voice; "I am your father."

In the thrust by which Harold had been made to stagger backward a little, the two men had got very near the long mirror. They were both white; both had anger and hatred in their faces; the hands of both were upraised. As Harold heard the last terrible words he started at the leaping throb that went through him, and in the start turned away from Jermyn. He turned it on the same face in the glass with his own beside it, and saw the hated fatherhood reasserted.

I, like Harold, felt the "leaping throb that went through," but I couldn't respond. Here was the man my parents least respected; the one I had been cautioned from youth not to be like; the one who, practically waltzing on my father's grave, was telling me that of all the people in the world, *he* was my father.

As if all this was not confusing enough, Abie now tossed a new bombshell. "I wouldn't be too disturbed. Because I may not be your father after all."

"No? Why not?"

"Well, Morris said that when he brought my semen to the office, the doctor mixed my semen with Morris's. So, who knows, you might actually still be Morris's son."

They mixed the semen? This seemed like a preposterous detail. Abie was surely making the whole thing up. He was delusional. This wasn't happening to me.

"But why didn't you tell me this before? Why didn't anyone tell me?"

"Morris made me swear never to say anything about this. I probably shouldn't even be telling you now. But you made me tell you."

"I *made* you? *You* told *me* you had a secret."

"Well, I shouldn't have told you."

This was degenerating into a squabble. I don't recall what I finally said. I just hung up the phone in a state of utter confusion.

I moved from the phone to the dining room table and collapsed into a chair, my head in my hands, sinking down to the table. As my eyes focused on the *New York Times* in front of me, I saw a headline: "New Use of Blood Test Is Decisive in Paternity Suits." The article talked about DNA paternity tests and how they could tell with 95 percent accuracy who your father really was. The coincidence made the information I had just received seem even more bizarre. Whose movie was I in?

In the days that followed, I had a virtual identity crisis, conjuring up how I would feel about my life if Abie was indeed my father. I would have to reenvision my whole childhood with this single but central fact in mind. I ran through many different scenarios, trying to imagine how my parents must have felt about me. Whenever my mother held me, kissed me, or just looked at me, was she thinking of me as Abie's son? Whenever my father reprimanded me or punished me, was he punishing the son of his problematic brother? All the times my parents told me not to be like Abie suddenly came to my mind. Why had I always had a sense of not belonging to my family? Although many kids have that feeling, now it seemed that my own perceptions had a special resonance. I didn't belong! I also, like many people, had a pervasive feeling of guilt, not for what I had done but simply for who I was. That began to make sense as well. Children are perceptive, and they pick up on emotions and situations without knowing exactly what they are. They get the feelings, if not the explanations for the feelings.

And then there was the constant and recurring dream I had been having for years. When the dream begins, I have committed a murder. I have disposed of the body by burying it in the dirt floor of the basement. No matter what I do or think in the dream, I can't escape the fact that I've buried a body in my cellar. When I wake up, it takes me several minutes to realize that, no, I haven't killed anyone. And no, I haven't buried anyone. But even after that I'm not really certain that this hasn't happened in the deep, dark past. Only after the sun comes up and rationality reasserts itself can I fully believe that I'm not a murderer. Whatever that dream means, it suggests some deep guilt buried in my past, some crime I've done that can't be undone and that I'm barely aware of having committed. Perhaps this buried secret of Abie's could account for the corpse that had somehow managed to find its way into my dream life.

After a few days, I began to feel a strange sense that my body wasn't my own but belonged to Abie. Like the character in the George Eliot novel, I began looking into the mirror and seeing Abie staring back at me. Abie was square, boxy, and heavy and had a visible dent in his skull where a childhood injury had caused harm—possibly brain damage. My brother and I had been told the injury had been caused by a hammer or some other blunt instrument to the head. My sense of my physical being had long been mentally linked with my father's body. Morris was thin and athletic with leg muscles that were long and stringy, as mine were. But when I looked at family photos, I saw that pictures of Abie as a young boy looked a lot like me. And photos of him at my age showed not a heavy, bulbous man but a thin, attractive one.

Torn between skepticism and belief, with Abie's unwelcome revelation never far from my mind, I felt as if the living uncle and the dead father were tugging my body in two directions. Since I had been taught to revile and be repulsed by my uncle from the earliest days of my childhood, I began to feel that way toward my own self. I'd look at my body in the mirror, see Abie in it, and feel a sense of disgust—it was like looking at a blurry photocopy of someone else, someone I didn't like.

As an academic, I reacted to this crisis by heading to the library. This was in the days before the Internet was a household word. I took the subway up to the Columbia University Medical Library on 168th Street. There I looked up "artificial insemination" to find out if the details that Abie provided could possibly be accurate. I discovered that artificial insemination with humans was just beginning to be written about in medical journals in the 1940s. I learned about the distinction between artificial insemination, which is the general description of the act of mechanically placing semen into a woman's vagina or uterus, and donor insemination, in which the semen comes from a man who is not the husband. An early article on donor insemination appeared in a British medical journal in 1945. I was born in 1949. The British article noted that "the husband's brother might be regarded as the first choice because of genotypical resemblance." So Abie might well have been the logical choice. The article was even more prescient when it noted that the problem with choosing a brother was that the choice was "usually incompatible with secrecy." My case surely proved this to be true.

I also found two articles from the *New York Times* about donor insemination. One from April 1945 detailed how Dr. Bernard Griffin, the archbishop of Westminster, appealed to a meeting of Roman Catholic doctors to oppose the production of "test tube babies" in Great Britain. These test tube babies weren't the products of the kind of high-tech in vitro fertilization practiced today, but were simply the equivalent of turkey baster babies. The article mentioned that "artificial insemination had been carried out at a clinic in Exeter" and quoted the archbishop as saying, "Such a practice offends against the dignity of man, sins against the laws of nature and is unjust to the offspring." And for good measure he added, "The act of the wife in receiving the seed of one who is not her husband has the malice of adultery." Had my parents felt they'd done some injustice to their offspring? And how did my mother feel with my uncle's seed growing in her? On some particularly dark day did she think that she had committed a form of adultery?

Another article from the *New York Times*, published thirteen days after I was born, carried the headline "Test Tube Practice Hit" followed by "Catholic Doctors Condemn Artificial Insemination." Four years after the first article, the Catholics were still at it. At a conference in Rome, Catholic doctors protested against this procedure, saying it was "contrary to the natural rules of parenthood." Professor Octave Pasteau of Paris said, "It would be frightful if one day we will have donors of human seed as popular as donors of blood." If only he knew.

But other views of test tube babies were more positive, indeed downright utopian. A proposal was made to the Military Affairs Committee of the House of Representatives in 1945 that "a super race of test-tube babies will become the guardians of the atom-bomb secrets.... Fathers will be chosen by eugenic experts of all the United Nations. The mothers will be handpicked on their health and beauty records, family background, and their achievements in school and university. The idea is to get the best possible brains in the world controlling future atomic power." It wasn't entirely clear how the mother's beauty and health would impact the decisions concerning the fate of the world, but I supposed such pleasing traits couldn't hurt.

My research also turned up the fact that in the early days of artificial insemination, doctors did, strangely enough, mix the semen together to make the infertile father feel better, because his DNA had at least a chance, however statistically insignificant, to get to the goal. As one expert wrote at the time, "The practice of mixing the semen of the husband with that of the donor is said, by those doctors who employ it, to have a psychological effect on the husband which is highly satisfactory... the chance, however small, that he is the father will do something to foster his self-esteem and evoke a sense of responsibility for the child." Another wrote, "For psychological purposes, many gynecologists add the husband's worthless semen to the donor's spermatozoa." So Abie had gotten the details right, although within a few years doctors would abandon the practice of mixing the donor semen with that of the infertile father, and would also begin using sperm mainly from anonymous donors.

In the midst of the depression that came over me as I struggled with the question of my paternity, my wife reminded me that my father—let's continue to call him that—was after all the person who had raised me, loved me, taken care of me. What did the DNA matter? Morris was my father. He taught me about life, and my experiences of his deafness in the hearing world shaped my sense of justice and perseverance. His artistic and athletic abilities gave me a direction for my own similar impulses.

In poking around my father's belongings during those days of uncertainty, I found a few things of interest. One was a play that he had written in longhand. I remembered, as I read it, that he had acted in it. My father and mother were part of a deaf club, and they often performed in theatrical events there. The play was about a Jewish father from the old country who is a tailor (as was my father) whose daughter begins secretly to go out with a Christian. When the father finds out about his daughter's love affair, he is distraught. But all turns out well in the end because the father discovers that the daughter isn't really his own child and is in fact actually the child of a Christian. The parallelism was too great. My father wrote a play in which his child turns out not to be his own. My father had played the part of the Jewish tailor in the deaf club performance. Art equals life?

I also found a notebook in which my father kept a record of his expenses. He was a bit of a miser and never trusted the idea of credit. As a result, he never had a checkbook and lived on a strictly cash basis. A methodical man, he recorded every item he bought, no matter how small: "rectal cream" for twenty-five cents. There, in the year of my birth, I found the name Max Sichell, who was the gynecologist who attended my mother during her labor, and surely the same man who would have performed the artificial insemination if it had occurred. I tried to contact him, but he had died, and his widow said his records had all gone to another physician, whose name she gave me. I tried calling him but kept getting a busy signal for two weeks. When I finally got through, I found that he, too, had just died. At that point, I gave up. Why was I pursuing this story with such vigilance when all the roads seemed to lead nowhere? I had a life; I had a growing family. I'd let sleeping fathers lie.

I accepted my wife's rationale that what mattered was that Morris had raised me, and I managed to put the whole business out of my mind until my daughter was born two years later. For the first week of her life I kept seeing Abie in her face and couldn't shake that feeling of a kind of haunting. Then the ghostly resemblance faded and my daughter Francesca's beautiful face became her own.

Four years after my father's death, Abie died. I hadn't had any contact with him during that time, or he with me. I did go to his funeral, which was a bizarre affair since there was almost no one there. When I walked into the room in some anonymous synagogue on Long Island only six other people were present: Abie's son, Leslie, with his wife, Marlene, and their son, Daniel; Abie's divorced second wife, Somdi; and an elderly couple from the old neighborhood in the Bronx where our families had lived when I was growing up. The rabbi, who did not know Abie, said a few general words of praise for a life that was not particularly praiseworthy. It reminded me of a joke about a man who had been such an awful person that no one could think of anything nice to say about him at his funeral. So there was total silence when the rabbi called on people to speak of the dead man. Finally one old guy gets up and says in desperation, "His brother was worse!" At Abie's funeral, no one made any such comparisons, although I made them in my mind.

After the funeral, I asked my cousin Les if he had ever heard anything relating to the story Abie had told me. He said he had never heard any such thing, and he assured me that he strongly doubted the truth of Abie's claims. He pointed out that he, his father, and his son all had bodies well endowed with birthmarks, while I did not. He also mentioned that Abie had been delusional at the time he called me, heard voices, and had to be committed to an institution for a spell shortly thereafter. I wasn't aware of any of this history. So was Abie just delusional in telling me that he was my father? Yet he had gotten the details right about the sperm being commingled. Perhaps he himself had tried out artificial insemination for Les, or he'd read about it a long time before. There was no way to know. In this story I was living there seemed to be no way to know anything for sure.

More years went by. I had mostly put the issue to rest. And then a few years ago, I thought about it again. I had written a memoir about my parents, *My Sense of Silence*, but hadn't included this dubious thread in the story. What I did include was my memory of an incident that occurred when I was about twelve or thirteen. My mother, my father, and I were all in the kitchen, my mother with her back to us as she bent over her ironing, when my father began telling me a story. When he was an adolescent in England, around 1910 or so, he said, he had contracted mumps. His testicles swelled up, and when the disease was over, he could feel that his left testicle was shrunken. He worried that he might be infertile. When he met my mother on a trip back to England, after he had become an American citizen, he didn't tell her about this state of affairs. During the two years that followed, they wrote to each other, my mother from Liverpool and my father from New York City, doing the entirety of their courting in letters. Finally, they agreed that she would come to the States and they would marry. It was then, my father told me, that he suddenly realized that he hadn't been honest with her. She would want to have babies, and he might not be able to impregnate her because of the mumps.

In addition to the mumps, my father may have been concerned about the possible consequences of having had a gonorrheal infection. He never told me this directly; the only grounds I have for thinking this is the sexual advice he gave me when I came of age. He told me to avoid promiscuous women and always use a condom, otherwise I might get gonorrhea, a word he spoke slowly with his difficult articulation while using the deaf sign language gestures for "pain" and "suffering." I'll never forget the look on his face when he signed those words, a look that told me he had experienced that pain.

My father determined to write his fiancée a letter confessing his potentially compromised fertility. He wrote about his fears and about his love for her, sealed the letter, and dropped it in the local mailbox. Walking slowly back to his Brooklyn apartment, he began to think over what he had just done. He feared that when my mother received the letter, she would call off the wedding. He loved her, and he realized that he had been too frank. He could lose her. So he ran back to the mailbox to wait for the letter carrier, but

Eva and Morris

when the box was opened, his letter wasn't there. No doubt it was already on its way to the Brooklyn borough post office. He then dashed down to that branch office only to find that the letter had already left and was on its way to the Manhattan central post office on Thirty-fourth Street. Here, most people would have let the matter go. But Morris was a person who was not to be deterred when he got an idea into his head.

He raced to the subway, got off at Thirty-fourth Street, and dashed up the imposing steps that rise to that granite-columned neoclassical building. It turns out that my father, in his scrupulous way, before addressing his letters to my mother, used to look up which ships were sailing to England. He would then write down the name of the ship on the front of the envelope, essentially telling the post office how to send his precious communication. When he approached the window in the grand post office, he was able to tell the clerk that his letter would be sailing on the S.S. *Elizabeth*, or whatever the ship may have been called, and he had to get the envelope back. He said it was "a matter of life or death." He must have made a strange sight, this wildly gesticulating, obviously hysterical deaf man with his guttural voice and insistent ways. But the wonder of the story is that he managed to get the letter back, and he destroyed it.

I was standing in the kitchen listening to this story as my father told it in sign language with much gesturing, facial expression, emotion, and detail. At the ripe old age of twelve, I felt myself fading away, like the boy in *Back to the Future*, when I heard of the letter heading toward my mother in England with my death sentence— never to have been born. And then I felt myself materializing back into my own being as my dad tore up the letter. Looking back at the story, which stuck in my head with incredible detail (I tell you this story at the age of fifty-eight, more than forty years later, and I feel like I'm in the kitchen listening to my father's every word and ASL sign), I realize now that he may have been on his way to telling me about the true circumstances of my birth. That would have been difficult for him, I am sure, and perhaps he lost his nerve and just left me with the setup. Or perhaps there was no further story. Or maybe something interrupted his telling of the story. My mother may have turned around from her ironing, piercing the bubble of privacy surrounding me and my father as he recounted those long ago events. And then the story was over.

As I mentioned, I included the story of my father and the letter in my memoir because I thought it was so revealing of his tenacity and determination, but I left out the further story of Abie and the secret. I wasn't ready to go public with that, and I didn't know how I felt about trying to uncover the truth. But now I felt ready.

So I contacted my cousin Les. We hadn't talked since his father's funeral fifteen years earlier. In the interim, I had met Les's son, Daniel, through a completely unrelated connection having to do with our mutual interest in disability studies, which is one of the subjects I now teach and write about. Daniel, who introduced himself to me one day when I was lecturing at the University of California at Berkeley, is a bright and likable young fellow. I asked Daniel if he knew anything about the Abie connection, and Daniel encouraged me to contact his father to ask him again. So when I called Les, he was ready. He told me that he had not gotten on with his father, considered him to have been abusive and crazy, and basically had not communicated with him much.

I reminded him of our last conversation years before. He recalled it and then added, "Look, I didn't tell you the truth last time."

"You didn't?"

"Last time you asked me, I tried to discourage you. I felt that you had just lost your father, and what was the point of disturbing you?"

"Disturbing me? What do you mean?"

"Well, I do know something about this. I have to tell you that my father did tell me the whole story. When I was twelve years old, he took me aside and said that he was your father. He told me everything. And he also told me never to tell you, and I had to swear I never would."

"So you knew but never told me? But what about the birthmarks and the hearing voices?"

"Well, that part was true."

I thought about Les and how he had always been nice to me when I was a kid. He was four years older than I was, and he would always bring me little presents and play with me. He was an only child whose mother had died young. I remember that he gave me a little gun that he said—and he had an odd sense of humor—was a pink elephant gun, only to be used on special occasions for the shooting of pink elephants. I didn't really understand what a pink elephant was, but I kept it in a treasured wooden cheese box where I stored my small toys. The gun was just a small thing, but I valued it highly. Now I wonder if perhaps he saw in me a younger brother, the brother he'd wanted but never had.

I remember going to the unveiling of his mother's tombstone, a ritual in which Jews return to the cemetery a year after the burial to erect a monument over the grave. I was about seven, and I recall my horror at seeing large water bugs and many-legged insects crawling in and out of the earth over her grave—it was my first realization of the reality of decomposition—and I also remember seeing Les crying inconsolably, which impressed me because I didn't know older boys cried.

I was astounded by Les's revelation. This new information now seemed to confirm Abie's story, and I had to give more credence to the idea that Abie was my father. But there was still an element of doubt. Abie could have imagined the whole story, and telling it to his son might have been a continuation of the delusion. Since he had been cruel to Les, perhaps this was another form of abuse. Having your father tell you that he has another, secret son might be a painful thing for any young boy to accept. And even if Abie had been telling the truth, there was also the mystery of the mixed semen. Perhaps one of my father's sperm really had made it to the finish line, as my father himself had done many times during his years as a champion race-walker. Although the fact that Les was now confirming his father's story was persuasive, I still held on to the hope that Abie's story was not true.

In a joke that seemed to sum up my dilemma, a man shows up at a detective agency and tells the detective, "I think my wife is having an affair, but I can't be sure. There's always this element of doubt." The detective assures the man that he'll get on the job and find out definitively. A week later the man returns to the detective's office. Now the detective has photographs. He says, "Here's a picture of you going off to work. Here's one of your wife going out of the house. Now here she's meeting a man at a bar, and you can see they are kissing each other. Then they go to a motel. I couldn't follow them in, but I have a telephoto shot I took through their window of them entering their motel room. See, they are kissing and ripping off their clothing. And then they close the curtains."

The man responds with frustration, "See, that's exactly what I mean...that *element of doubt!*"

I found myself now in that situation. I could try to track down testimonies and recollections, but would I ever have final proof? In a way, I was engaged in what nineteenth-century psychiatrists called a *"folie à doute,"* doubting mania, in which I'd ask myself a million questions, provide answers to them, but always find something more to doubt.

It might occur to you to say, "Why doesn't this man just accept what his uncle told him and his cousin confirmed?" That might seem compelling to someone who wasn't living this story. But for me the desire for some corroborating proof had become a kind of obsession. It was as if two lawyers were arguing the case in my head, and I had to track down the evidence that would decide the case one way or the other. It would no doubt be hard to find that evidence. Even if Abie's story was true, it could also have been true that Morris was my father, because one of his sperm might have made it to the egg.

To find an answer and work through my obsession, I decided to read everything I could find about artificial and donor insemination. Perhaps somewhere in that history I could discover some clues about my existence.

I have become convinced by the nature of things that nothing per se can be regarded as incredible.

—PLINY, QUOTED BY LAZARO SPALLANZANI,
EIGHTEENTH-CENTURY PRIEST WHO WAS THE FIRST
SCIENTIST TO ARTIFICIALLY INSEMINATE A MAMMAL

TWO

A *Natural History of Artificial Insemination*

THE YEAR WAS 1884. Amanda, thirty-one, a Quaker married to a merchant ten years her senior, was nervous and preoccupied. She had been trying to conceive a child for several years but had remained childless. Her marriage had become strained as she and her husband felt their parental birthright stolen from them by some unseen and malicious force. Amanda had repeatedly sought help from her doctor, William Pancoast, a professor at Jefferson Medical College in Philadelphia and a physician who was so highly regarded that he had been asked to perform the autopsy on the celebrated Siamese twins Chang and Eng. Despite his fame and ability, Dr. Pancoast had not been able to help. Even after extensive testing, he could find nothing wrong with Amanda. These tests were so thorough they included mechanically inducing an orgasm in her and then watching the suction of the uterus. Every part of her seemed to be working just fine.

On this visit to her doctor she was desperate. He had told her that this was to be her last consultation. After this try, there would be no hope. When Amanda arrived, she was discomfited to see a group of eight men gathered together whispering with the physician. Dr. Pancoast introduced them as his medical students. She felt embarrassed by the frank way in which they looked at her. The doctor asked her to go to another room, remove her clothing, and don a hospital gown. When she returned, she lay down on an examining table. Dr. Pancoast told her he would be giving her something to make her go to sleep while he conducted his examination.

When Amanda awoke, she was alone with a nurse. On the way home, Amanda felt dispirited. But a month later she found she was pregnant. In due time, a child, a boy, was born, and she and her husband were delighted.

What Amanda did not know was that Dr. Pancoast had determined the problem lay with her husband, who had no sperm in his semen, a condition that probably resulted from a bout of gonorrhea. So the doctor decided on a radical course—to artificially impregnate her with the semen of a "hired man." Dr. Pancoast had suggested that the "best-looking" student contribute his semen. The semen had then been put into a hard rubber syringe and injected into Amanda's uterus, after which her cervix was plugged up with a wad of gauze. No one told her what had occurred, and only when the pregnancy was certain did Dr. Pancoast inform the husband. He, in turn, agreed not to tell Amanda, and so the secret was kept until one of the students, Addison Davis Hard, published a letter twenty-five years later in the journal *Medical World*, after the death of Dr. Pancoast, revealing what he called the first case of artificial impregnation in a human. Hard, residing by this time in California, even went to meet the result of this medical procedure, now twenty-five years old and living in New York. (Hard's commitment to assessing the outcome of an experiment of a quarter century before suggests that Hard himself might well have been the "best-looking" student.)

Hard, in his article, went so far as to recommend that artificial insemination be used as the routine and normal form of reproduction instead of sexual intercourse. Basing his reasoning on eugenics, the new "science" of improving human beings by better breeding, he concluded that since the offspring of the experiment was now a successful businessman, this was an argument in favor of eugenically engineered pregnancies. After all, he said, the origin of the semen was not very important, only the outcome. "Origin of spermatozoa which generates the ovum is not more important than the finger which pulls the trigger of a gun." And since, according to Hard, one man out of five had a venereal disease (at least in New York City), these inseminations would help to protect their wives from potential infection.

The founder of eugenics was a smart, handsome British man named Francis Galton, a cousin of Charles Darwin. Galton was a medical student who dropped out of university when he had a nervous breakdown. He spent the rest of his life on a series of intellectual forays that at various times saw him studying statistics, exploring Africa, inventing fingerprinting, developing methods of measuring time, and promoting his ideas about the use of selective breeding for the improvement of the human race. While Galton himself didn't advocate artificial insemination, his followers developed an interest in eliminating defective fathers by using the semen of "superior" men to develop a race of geniuses and athletic marvels. Both Stalin and Hitler would later put scientists to work on eugenics experiments designed to develop a master race, while the United States and Britain advocated a form of eugenic planning that would encourage "fitter" members of society to marry each other.

Although Dr. Pancoast's successful impregnation of Amanda is widely regarded as the first documented case of human donor insemination, there are a number of earlier accounts of artificial insemination in which the husband's own sperm was inserted via mechanical means into his wife. One of the few to have been reported prior to the nineteenth century occurred in 1785 when Scottish physician John Hunter advised artificial insemination to help a linen draper with hypospadia, a condition in which the opening of the penis is at the base rather than the tip. The man in question was able to have sex with his wife, but the ejaculate would dribble out the bottom of his member rather than entering the vaginal canal. Hunter provided the husband with a syringe, advising him to use it to collect his semen immediately after intercourse and then insert it into the vagina "while the female organs were still under the influence of the coitus and in the proper state for receiving the semen." The husband did as he was told, and his wife bore a child.

Interestingly, the first documented case of artificial insemination in a nonhuman mammal occurred not long before, in 1780, when Lazaro Spallanzani, an Italian priest and professor at the University of Pavia who had been experimenting with the fertilization of reptiles, decided to move on to dogs. He had been wondering if he could apply the skills he had learned in fertilizing the eggs of frogs, salamanders, and toads, whose eggs are fertilized outside of their bodies, to animals who were fertilized by internal insemination. As he wrote, "I cogitated these problems for a considerable time and could not get them out of my head. . . . In 1780 I decided to try it out on a spaniel bitch that had had a litter before." What might have been considered an indecent obsessive thought became the foundation of artificial insemination—which the Catholic Church itself would later ban.

Spallanzani waited until the dog "showed signs of coming into heat" and then locked her up, keeping the key on his person and being the only one to feed her so that he could ensure her isolation. He waited for thirteen days until he "saw clear signs of heat, the external sex organs becoming moist and excreting engorged fluid." He continued to wait until he deemed her "ready for artificial fecundation." He obtained nineteen grains of seminal fluid "by spontaneous ejaculation [of] a young dog of the same breed [and] . . . I immediately injected [it] into the uterus by means of a syringe." Spallanzani realized that the temperature of the semen was crucial to its viability, so he made sure that the syringe was kept at the temperature of the dog's body. "After two days I saw that she was no longer in heat and after twenty days that her belly was swollen." The dog gave birth to three pups, two males and a female. One side discovery made by Spallanzani was that because "six grains of seminal fluid had remained behind in the syringe," it must be that "a very small amount of semen is required in nature [for fertilization]."

Spallanzani's discovery prompted Charles Bonnet, the Swiss naturalist who discovered parthenogenesis, to write to him and predict, "I am not so sure but that what you have just discovered may not some day have consequences for mankind of no mean significance." Ironically, this bald and pleasant-faced man sworn to celibacy ended up helping the world to a better understanding of sex.

Much of the early experimentation on human insemination was done in France. In 1838 a Dr. Girault used a method he called "insufflation," in which a rubber instrument was moistened with semen and then the contents were blown into the neck of the uterus. Within a period of thirty years he attempted ten *fécondations artificielles*," of which eight were successful. Another doctor, François Dehaut, used to perform his inseminations with a crystal tube about eight inches long. In 1846, a Dr. Gigon used a long celluloid catheter through which he introduced semen into the womb. He would have the husband fill a glass tube with semen in an adjoining room, and then Dr. Gigon connected the glass tube to the catheter and streamed the semen into the waiting wife's vagina.

While there were a number of these haphazard and occasional attempts during the early years of artificial insemination, the latter half of the nineteenth century ushered in a more systematic approach. The first repeated and controlled set of inseminations was performed by Dr. J. Marion Sims, who is widely considered the founder of American gynecology, having established the first hospital for women in New York City. From 1866 to 1868 he attempted approximately fifty-five uterine injections on half a dozen couples in London and Paris. Sims had gained fame for his cure of the previously incurable vesicovaginal fistula, a painful, disabling, and debilitating disease that was the result of traumatic childbirth. He also invented a gynecological device that evolved into the currently used speculum. Though in recent years the revelation that he perfected his surgical techniques and devices on his black slaves without anesthesia or consent has turned his fame to notoriety, during his own era he was considered a leader in his field.

Ever open to new endeavors, he decided to try his hand at artificial insemination and to use a technique that varied from those used before. While husband and wife had sexual intercourse, Sims waited in an adjoining room. After the husband's ejaculation, Sims entered the room, removed the seminal fluid from the wife's vagina, and, using an instrument of his own devising, injected a drop of the semen directly into the uterus via a device powered by a piston. In one instance, Sims injected semen into a woman whom he characterized as having a "hyperesthetic" vagina. Presumably the woman could not tolerate sexual intercourse, and so Sims used ether to render her senseless while inseminating her with her husband's semen. He called this procedure "etherized copulation." Sims reported conception rates of 4 percent, considerably lower than current rates of 20 percent, no doubt because Sims, along with most experts of the day, believed that ovulation occurred during menstruation. The very limited understanding of the biology of human sexual reproduction in combination with the queasiness that many people felt about artificial insemination kept the procedure from catching on. Sims eventually came to regard insemination as an "immoral medical practice" and never performed it again.

Some of Sims's contemporaries came to a similar conclusion. One early French physician named Roubaud objected to Sims's procedure saying that "the carrying out of this operation immediately after coitus is bound to exercise a very unfavorable moral effect, particularly upon the woman. At the very moment in which the woman is still quivering in the last throes of the orgasm, the physician is to enter the bedroom with a syringe in hand." Roubaud considered the Sims method "too American" because it took no account of a woman's feeling of shame. (Interesting that the French should fault the Americans for being insufficiently prudish!) Another contemporary, the well-known German sexologist Dr. Hermann Rohleder, objected to Sims's technique, saying that he "went too far in his attempt to help his patient . . . In my view, even in the laudable effort to help, a physician should not give up his self-respect and should not engage in practices the characterization of which our written language does not have proper words for."

But artificial insemination did have its proponents. Edward Bliss Foote, a popular U. S. writer on sexuality whose books *Medical Common Sense* and *Plain Home Talk* were widely read during the second half of the nineteenth century, advocated the use of an "impregnating syringe" (which he sold by mail order) in cases where the cervix was abnormal. He went further than Sims, who used only the husband's semen, when he wrote that if the husband's fluids were found to be devoid of spermatozoa, "the male germs must be obtained" from a donor other than the husband.

Dr. Robert L. Dickinson began performing donor inseminations in the 1890s but, fearing public reaction, did not publicly let it be known until the 1930s. We can assume that there must have been other doctors performing artificial or even donor insemination at the time, but there surely weren't many of them, and most doctors didn't approve of the procedures.

The interest in artificial insemination also had a eugenic component, as discussed, and not just as part of a Stalinist plot to build a better warrior or the Hitlerian goal of achieving ethnically pure citizens. J.B.S Haldane, who pioneered population genetics, came out with a book called *Daedalus* in 1924, that proposed "ectogenesis," the breeding of children in test tubes, using the sperm and eggs of the best men and women of their time. Haldane, a devilishly handsome man with a handlebar moustache, was a friend and collaborator of Julian Huxley, the scientist and older brother of Aldous Huxley. In *Brave New World*, the dystopian novel by Aldous Huxley published in 1932, the centerpiece of Huxley's vision of the future is a huge laboratory in which children are conceived through artificial insemination and gestated in vitro—in a world in which love and sexuality are separated from reproduction, just as Haldane had suggested. Huxley himself was horrified by the world he envisioned and most particularly by this aspect of it. But Haldane's call for "ectogenesis" was part of a whole movement of utopian-minded scientists, and it was soon seconded by biologist H. J. Muller. His 1935 manifesto *Out of the Night: A Biologist's View of the Future* said of Haldane's suggestions: "Such an advance in reproduction would be valuable in affording us a much more direct control over the development of the embryo; but...it would be even more valuable in enabling us to rear selectively—or even to multiply—those embryos which have received a superior heredity."

Muller, who had been hired by Julian Huxley to teach biology at Rice University, also advocated reproduction via artificial insemination, which already by 1935 he viewed as a procedure that was "tried and proved." Using the sperm of some "transcendentally estimable man" in a series of artificial inseminations would allow mass reproduction of "positive" genes "without either of the parents concerned ever having come in contact with or even seen each other, or having been in any way disturbed in their separate personal and family lives...Only social inertia and popular ignorance now hold us back from putting into effect...such a severance of the function of reproduction from the personal love-life of the individual." Muller also predicted the possibility of preserving sperm for use after the death of an individual, and recommended waiting twenty-five years before using it so that society could have the benefit of hindsight to decide whether or not the man had indeed been great. A communist and materialist, he then added, "How fortunate we should be had such a method been in existence in time to have enabled us to secure living cultures of some of our departed great. How many women, in an enlightened community devoid of superstitious taboos and of sex slavery, would be eager and proud to bear and rear a child of Lenin or Darwin!"

Interest in the eugenic advantages of artificial insemination grew steadily through the 1930s and 1940s thanks in part to the inhuman and profoundly unethical experiments of Nazi scientists. In the late 1930s, more than three hundred Jewish women at Auschwitz were kept in the infamous Cell Block 10, run by Dr. Carl Clauberg, who artificially inseminated many of them. Indeed, Hitler's plans for a eugenically perfect and ethnically "pure" citizenry could be seen as a natural outgrowth of all these earlier discussions on the part of the English, Russian, and American scientists and physicians.

By 1934 there had been enough experiments in insemination

to warrant the publication of a history of the procedure. Titled *Test Tube Babies: A History of the Artificial Impregnation of Human Beings*, it was written by sexologist Dr. Hermann Rohleder, author of an earlier work advocating human-chimp hybrids (as a way of learning more about humans and our evolutionary past), who claimed that his new book was "the only history of artificial impregnation of human beings ever written," and at the time it probably was. Rohleder opens the book by marveling that "although the operation is so easy that it can be carried out by practically every physician, the medical profession generally . . . is almost as ignorant of it as the laity who, by and large, do not even suspect the existence of such a method." Rohleder notes that he tried artificial insemination, which he called "artificial fecundation," in nineteen cases and was successful in five. And he adds that he wrote the book to "espouse the cause of this operation and fight for its honor."

For the "operation" to work, according to Rohleder, the woman must be sexually aroused. He notes that "no responsible physician would take" that route and so the couple must have had sex immediately before the doctor performs the insemination. He goes on:

My procedure in this operation is as follows. . . . [The husband,] to save the modesty of the woman . . . is directed to have intercourse with a condom at a definite hour, if possible on the last day of his wife's menstruation. . . . Shortly after the coitus . . . has been enacted, the physician appears. The woman remains in bed, lying upon her back; her pelvic girdle is raised somewhat by placing pillows under the small of the back. Then the physician with the assistance of the husband (indeed I would not advise carrying out this operation save in his presence) introduces a vaginal speculum.... Then as quickly as possible, a clean dry... syringe...is inserted into the condom; a little semen is aspirated, the syringe is introduced into the cervical canal about two centimeters, and slowly a few drops are injected.... At the mouth of the womb is placed a pad of cotton that has been thoroughly wetted with semen and provided with a long string. The woman's knees are then tied together with a towel and she is directed to avoid all movement. Furthermore, she is ordered to remain in bed for the next few hours and preferably for the remainder of the day.

This is the first detailed description we have of how to do artificial insemination, and it is riddled with errors. Women don't have to be sexually aroused to conceive, and obviously they are not fertile during or immediately after their periods. It is also interesting to note that Rohleder's technique is quite similar to that of Sims, whose entry into the marital chamber Rohleder and other physicians had objected to on moral grounds. Here Rohleder saves the woman's honor by having the husband use a condom, which meant that the physician did not have to retrieve the semen from the vagina.

Rohleder's mistakes may amuse us, but the rather incredible fact is that it wasn't until the 1930s that the full story of human reproduction emerged, and it wasn't until some time after that that the facts became widely known. Even the greatest intellectuals and writers of the nineteenth and early twentieth centuries—people such as Karl Marx, Charles Darwin, Charles Dickens, George Eliot, and Sigmund Freud—did not have the understanding of human reproduction that the typical high school student today has.

If you try to forget everything you've learned about the birds and the bees, you'll see that it would have been almost impossible, especially before good-quality microscopes, to have come up with the idea of sperm and egg coming together to form a child. Before the age of the microscope, having heard some theories that proposed that semen was "seed," you might have been familiar with the idea that somehow sexual intercourse led to babies, but you'd also have heard other theories maintaining that the seed was scattered around the environment and just happened to come into men and women through food or even breath. Virgil, in this translation by Dryden, attributed the generative process to the air, justifying this by noting that mares could be impregnated by the wind.

> *The Mares to Cliffs of rugged Rocks repair,*
> *And, with wide Nostrils, snuff the Western Air;*
> *When (wondrous to relate) the Parent Wind,*
> *Without the Stallion, propagates the Kind.*

The Greek physician Hippocrates believed that a man and a woman both produced sperm, and that if they both produced strong versions of sperm, then a male was born, while if both produced weak sperm, a female was born. Aristotle and his followers believed that it was the heat from the man's semen that triggered the female organs to create a baby on their own. In postclassical times, the virgin birth of Jesus presupposes that at least under divine circumstances sexual intercourse was not necessary for reproduction, and the Jewish Talmud records a discussion in which the famous second-century rabbi Ben Zoma allows for the possibility that a virgin could have a child without a man.

The early Christian writer Tertullian believed that it was the soul itself that produced semen in both men and women:

> In a single impact of both parties, the whole human frame is shaken and foams with semen, in which the damp humor of the body is joined to the hot substance of the soul. . . . I cannot help asking, whether we do not, in that very heat of extreme gratification when the generative fluid is ejected, feel that somewhat of our soul has gone out from us? And do we not experience a faintness and prostration along with a dimness of sight? This then, must be the soul producing seed, which arises from the outdrip of the soul, just as that fluid is the body-producing seed which proceeds from the drainage of the flesh.

Absent scientific proof, various theories of conception abounded through the centuries that followed. Many people believed that the male's semen included a "homunculus," a little man, which was implanted in the woman, who was merely a vessel.

But one idea that had never occurred to anyone before the seventeenth century was that women, like chickens and frogs, had eggs, while men had tiny, invisible tadpole-like animals with large heads and whipping tails, and that the coming together of the two created a child. Such a theory would have been laughable.

Demonstrable proof of this theory of human reproduction first began with the speculations of a tradesman in Delft. An unlikely prospect as a scientist on the cutting edge of biological research, Antoni van Leeuwenhoek was a pleasant-faced if doughy-looking man who owned a small fabric store in the Netherlands. He was a man without family fortune or university degree, who spoke only Dutch. Coming from such humble origins, he didn't embark on his scientific investigations until much later in life. Sometime around 1668, Leeuwenhoek took up, perhaps as a hobby, the art of lens grinding and turned out to be rather extraordinary at it. While others had already used lenses to examine the tiny things of nature, Leeuwenhoek managed to make much better lenses and, with his highly acute vision, applied himself with great zeal to his microscopic observations. He didn't invent the microscope per se, but he did the best job of seeing the virtually invisible.

Leeuwenhoek's microscope was surprisingly small, just about the size of a postage stamp, with a lens smaller than a lentil. The object to be investigated was placed on a sharp metallic point just below the lens, and screws brought the object into focus. His microscope was essentially just a very good single magnifying glass, which could enlarge objects anywhere from 200 to possibly 550 times. How amazing to think that Leeuwenhoek, with this relatively simple and crude instrument, was able to observe and describe for the first time in history bacteria, protozoa, and, most important to our subject, human sperm.

It was actually a medical student named Johan Ham who in 1677 told Leeuwenhoek that he had seen tiny animalcules in human seminal fluid. Ham brought Leeuwenhoek what he described as "the spontaneously discharged semen of a man who had lain with an unclean woman and was suffering from gonorrhea." Ham thought that animalcules, literally "little animals," were present in the semen because of either the gonorrhea or simply the fact that the semen was putrefying. But Leeuwenhoek made detailed drawings of these creatures and attributed their existence not to putrefaction or disease but to the normal mechanics of reproduction. Leeuwenhoek speculated that the animalcules contained the completely formed human, the homunculus of earlier speculation, which was then simply deposited in the uterus to be nourished by the female. Apparently, the discovery of these spermatozoa caused so much publicity that King Charles II himself wanted to go and have a look at the wriggling marvels.

Although Leeuwenhoek wasn't a scientist in a traditional sense and did not write articles about his findings, he did send letters containing detailed descriptions of what he had seen to the Royal Society in London, an organization that was the premier institution for scientific advancement in all of Europe. It is in a letter of November 1677 that he recounted how he had discovered living spermatozoa in human semen and accurately described their movement and their size.

Despite his observations, it took a long time for his work to be accepted. As Leeuwenhoek wrote to a friend, "I know very well that there are Universities who do not believe that living creatures are in the male semen; but I do not mind about this, as I know I have the truth."

By late in the seventeenth century, one very popular book about sex, called *Aristotle's Masterpiece*—although it had nothing to do with the Greek philosopher—conjured up the notion of "seed" from both male and female. The book enjoyed a shelf life of about two hundred years, despite being rife with misinformation. *Aristotle's Masterpiece* offers us an excellent window into how common folks of the time viewed reproduction. Menstrual flow is equated with fertility, and the book talks about the man's seed as being made from frothed blood and animal spirits. The woman's seed—which in some versions of the book is referred to as the "ovum" or egg—is located in her "ovaries," also called "stones" or even "testicles." This may be one of the earliest mentions in print of the human female having "eggs." Conception occurs in the womb, not the fallopian tubes, and if a woman lies on her right side after intercourse, her heat on that side of the uterus (which is called the "matrix") will cause a male child to be formed, while lying on the left side will gestate a female. Because both men and women produce seed, their reproductive parts are seen as mirror versions of each other. As one poetic section of *Aristotle's Masterpiece* puts it, talking about women (to a presumed male reader):

> ... that, tho' they of different Sexes be,
> Yet in the whole they are the same as we:
> For those that have the strictest Searchers been,
> Find Women are but Men turn'd Out side in:
> And Men, if they but cast their Eyes about,
> May find they're Women, with their Inside out.

After Leeuwenhoek's studies, the next major step in discovering how reproduction occurred took place more than a century and a half later. Karl Ernst von Baer, a man with a Hapsburg jaw, a huge nose, and a bad comb-over, was a Prussian knight who was also a professor of biology and zoology at Königsberg University and later at the St. Petersburg Academy of Sciences. Although in later years he would become an ardent critic of Darwin and the idea of evolution, during the early part of his career he made a major (if now little remembered) discovery, which has earned him a permanent place in the annals of biology. Von Baer was the first to confirm the existence of the mammalian ovum—in the ovaries of a dog. While this may seem a small accomplishment, remember that although many, including the British physician William Harvey, discoverer of the circulation of blood, had speculated that mammals had eggs, just as birds, insects, and fish did, no one before von Baer had been able to see them. Mammalian eggs, like sperm, are microscopic, but unlike sperm they are very hard to find, which explains why the fact that mammals (including humans) have eggs remained speculation for such a long time.

Remember also that the scientific discoveries of the past were not hailed in newspapers, flashed on television screens, or deployed on the Internet. Often a physician might publish his or her research in a pamphlet that would lie dormant for years or just wither on the information vine. So in 1826 there were no kudos or instant fame for von Baer and his discovery. Knowledge of the mammalian ovum and its function did not sweep the world, or even Europe, and the set of explanations that we now have about sex was still a long way off in the future. It would in fact require the passing of yet another century (plus a few years) before anyone found and documented the extremely tiny human egg.

Even the word *conception* is relatively new, coined by Dr. Martin Barry in 1843. In that year he was able to document that rabbit sperm had penetrated a rabbit ovum. But in general, the nineteenth century remained in ignorance of the way that fertilization took place, and there were many inaccurate ideas. For example, it was generally believed that the human egg was only released through sexual intercourse, and it wasn't until midcentury that this myth was debunked. Well into the twentieth century, most researchers held the opinion that for fertilization to take place, a woman had to have an orgasm accompanying the fertilization. As one eighteenth-century doctor put it, "the womb must be in a state of delight" or the sexual encounter would be fruitless from the point of view of reproduction.

People in the nineteenth and even the early twentieth century were uncertain whether conception took place in the uterus or the ovaries, and didn't even consider the fallopian tubes, which of course is where fertilization does take place. Although they knew about the spermatozoa in semen, they weren't sure what exactly the sperm did. A physician in 1909, echoing an opinion going back to Aristotle that the male's contribution is less important than the female's, wrote that sperm was merely something that "generates the ovum," providing a kind of accelerant to the egg, which went on to develop more or less on its own. According to him, "the mother is the complete builder of the child...her blood gives material for the body...the tendencies and mental caliber of the child."

In 1905 Theodoor van de Velde made the discovery that a woman normally releases only one egg per month rather than several, as was earlier believed. But it wasn't until the 1920s that two doctors, Hermann Knaus of Austria and Kyusaku Ogino of Japan, independently arrived at the now obvious conclusion that human women were fertile not during menstruation, like dogs, but two weeks after the cessation of their periods. These researchers also noted a basal temperature shift that would identify when ovulation took place—an observation that allowed Dutch Catholic physician John Smulders to create the rhythm method of contraception in 1930.

But the discoveries of Knaus and Ogino, like so many others in this area, took a long time to infiltrate even into professional consciousness. A full ten years after Ogino's and Knaus's work, the sexologist Rohleder could write in 1934 in *Test Tube Babies*, "It is a well-known fact that fertilization is easier during menstruation than otherwise." He noted that many women might object on the grounds of cleanliness, and that for Orthodox Jews this advice "will create dismay" since the Talmud forbids coitus during menstruation. But Rohleder was wrong and the Jews were right after all.

The human egg was one of the most elusive objects in modern science. Only in 1930 was the human ovum finally seen and documented by the embryologist Edgar Allen. And, amazingly, the first high-quality photographs of the human ovum would not appear until 1960, when Landrum Shettles, who pioneered in vitro fertilization, published his book *Ovum Humanum*. Photographs of human conception itself had to wait until 1965, when Lennart Nilsson published his pictures in a book titled (in the English edition that appeared the year after the original Swedish edition)

A Child Is Born. What all this means is that humans did not "see" conception until a little over four decades ago.

As the facts of life became known and in a sense less mysterious, doctors began to perform artificial inseminations more frequently and, not surprisingly, more successfully, as their knowledge had led to better techniques and more accurate timing. For the first time, medicine could go public and offer childless couples a chance to conceive. Now it was less a question of whether artificial insemination could work and more a problem of informing the general public about the opportunities.

In the United States, Dr. Frances Seymour and her husband, Dr. Alfred Koerner, who tirelessly promoted the procedure, did much to further the cause of donor insemination. In fact, one of the first media events surrounding the making of what were called at the time "test tube babies," a term applied to both artificial and donor insemination, involved Seymour and an Italian American couple. Salvatore and Lillian Lauricella approached Dr. Seymour after Lillian had undergone various fertility treatments and failed to conceive. The problem, it turned out, was that Salvatore's semen had no spermatozoa. Seymour saw this case as an excellent vehicle for getting publicity for donor insemination. After several tries with semen from an anonymous donor, Lillian became pregnant and eventually gave birth on April 17, 1934, to twin daughters. The story was widely reported in the press, including an article in the *New York Times* headlined "'Synthetic' Babies Born to 12 Mothers: 'Laboratory Twins' Are Among Offspring Here of Previously Childless Persons."

At the time, most U.S. physicians still opposed artificial insemination of any kind, according to a survey done by *Scientific American*. Of the 200 doctors who were interviewed for the survey, 129 reported they discouraged the practice, 56 said they had received requests for the procedure, and only 22 agreed to carry it out. So just one out of ten doctors considered performing artificial insemination—and that was with the husband's semen. How many fewer would have approved it if it was done with donor semen? In the same year, Hermann Rohleder, who favored artificial insemination using the husband's sperm but not that of a stranger, wrote: "What husband or wife, no matter how intense their longing for an heir, will consent to an injection of strange semen? Thank God that most people still have that much tact, decency, and moral feeling." Dr. C. T. Stepita wrote in 1933 that he thought it was wrong to use a syringe with donor semen because "knowledge of the fact this semen comes from a stranger is distressing to and bad for the wife." So he had developed the rather complex procedure of catheterizing the infertile husband's ejaculatory ducts and then injecting the donor's semen directly into them. The husband then had sexual intercourse with his wife, she none the wiser, and the husband ejaculated the donor's semen from his own penis into his wife's vagina. This technique must have been wildly uncomfortable and so, for fairly obvious reasons, did not catch on.

In 1941, Seymour and Koerner published a highly influential article about artificial insemination in the *Journal of the American Medical Association*. The article, which noted the exponential increase in the number of children born as a result of artificial insemination, caused an uproar and resulted in a public debate about the morality of the procedure. Doctors such as Alan Guttmacher, who was president of Planned Parenthood, became major supporters of the technology, seeing it as part of an overall plan to give parents and doctors more control over reproduction. In that same year, one survey estimated that ten thousand pregnancies had been brought about by artificial insemination, two-thirds of which used the husband's semen alone. If the survey was accurate, that means that by 1941, about thirty-three hundred babies had been conceived by donor insemination.

Within the same decade, if what Abie said was true, I would join their numbers.

THREE

Keywords from Childhood

Something Wrong

I spent my whole childhood feeling something was wrong. Of course, I had the obvious "something wrong"—both my parents were deaf. So if I thought about it, I could pin a lot of what I thought was wrong onto that donkey, and it was a pretty large donkey. But if you grow up in a family with disabilities, the disabilities melt away into what simply feels like a normal family setting. Sure, my parents were deaf, but then weren't all parents to a greater or lesser degree?

No, the something wrong was more on the order of a feeling that was unspoken, in sign language or any other language. There was a steady *basso continuo*, an underlying murmur, of something that was awry in our world. A lot of what seemed to be wrong had to do with my father, but my mother also lived in the world of something wrong, albeit in a different way.

My father, Morris Joseph Davis, was a dark, lanky, handsome man with a bald head, a pencil-thin moustache, and a dangerous

Morris

way in the world. He was born in 1898 and had something Victorian about him, a severity in his approach to raising children, and something primitive in him, too, as if his sensibilities had been formed before the car, the telephone, and movies—perhaps even bronze—were invented. In our house, you wanted to steer clear of him. But since our house was a one-bedroom apartment in the Bronx, you couldn't steer very clear of him. He was a moody man, prone to fits of rage, but also capable of humor and hijinks. He was like uncertain weather. With him you never knew whether to dress for storm or sunshine. When he was sunny, the world was a lot of fun. He liked to mimic Charlie Chaplin and he could play with me on my own level, since, in a way, we were both children. But then, like a child, he could erupt into willful tantrums. He was rarely physically abusive—although he did spank us, and he used to whip my brother with a cat-o'-three-tails—but he was often verbally abusive (in sign language) and seemed to enjoy humiliating and ridiculing us. Although Morris was my father, sometimes he seemed more like the stepfather you'd read about in Dickens's novels. And yet he was not entirely hateful, not a villain, just not the right dad for me.

My mother, Eva, was a pretty woman who had had a good deal of the inner life crushed out of her, partly by her lot in life and partly by living with my father. She became deaf when she was seven, having contracted spinal meningitis. She was a hardworking woman who sewed at home, doing alterations for the women in the neighborhood. I could make her laugh, but mostly she was quietly depressed. She seemed happiest when she was with her deaf female friends or when she was with me. She was my confidante and soul mate, and I loved to talk with her, asking her about her childhood, and to help her cook and clean. I was the daughter she always wanted, only I was her son.

What was wrong? I knew that my mother had always wanted a daughter because she told me this practically every day. I was happy to be a boy, but I definitely registered her unhappiness at being daughterless. As a seamstress, she made many of her own clothes, and always wished she could make dresses for me. How I managed to avoid being a transvestite is a kind of mystery to me now.

I never liked my father, although I loved him, as Cordelia did Lear, according to my bond: no more, no less. I never felt I was his favorite. That dubious distinction went to my older brother, Gerald. Ten years older than me, Gerald seemed a more entrenched part of my parents' family, while I always felt like the outsider. Gerald was groomed to become what my father could never have been himself—a doctor. As it played out, Gerald didn't become a doctor, either. But back then he was expected to be the living antidote to my father's limitations, a burden that I now see was in a way worse than being what I thought I was—an extraneous child, the extra boy.

As soon as I understood there were things called books, I lived to be read to. I can still recall the seductive smell and alluring pictures that pulled me into a page like a lost traveler finding a snug place for the night. My favorite book, which I would ask any hapless person gullible enough to succumb to my pleas to read to me over and over again, was *The Ugly Duckling*. I was sure I was that ugly duckling, put in the wrong nest, full of beauty and talent that were unrecognized by my father, in particular, because I wasn't the duck he wanted me to be. I didn't quack his quack or waddle his walk. My father was very athletic, a world-class race-walker, and I was a neurasthenic runt who liked to read. In the child's tale of the cygnet placed among lesser fowl, the dominant emotion is humiliation, pain, rejection, which changes to joy once the rejected bird, having endured in a marsh all winter, is reunited come spring with his own kind, and flies off at last in triumph as a member of the elegant squadron of swans.

But I never was able to find my own kind in my family. Something was wrong. Why didn't I fit?

You can tell a lot about a kid by the games he or she plays. One of my favorite games, which my brother and I invented, was called "Counterspy." This game would be played in the dark hours of winter before dinner was served, and it involved my father as he lay asleep in an armchair in the living room. My father spent a lot of his life sleeping. Because he worked seasonally in the garment district, he was home about half the year—time he spent collecting unemployment insurance, reading the newspaper, giving us the eagle eye, and then falling asleep. He'd fall asleep at the table reading the newspaper—the *Daily News*, New York's working-class newspaper and scandal rag. He'd fall asleep sitting on the couch. But most frequently he'd fall asleep in his favorite slipcovered armchair by the window next to the guppy tank and the calendar commemorating the coronation of Queen Elizabeth with its adjustable knobs for the day and the date. The game Gerald and I played always took place in the semidarkness of the living room as dusk fell and my mother cooked dinner. My brother and I would crawl on the floor toward our snoring father. Our Cold War–inspired fantasy was that he was actually a Russian spy and we were American counterspies. Although he seemed to have the perfect alibi—his cover being that he was a poor Jewish deaf immigrant living in the Bronx, someone the CIA would never suspect—we knew better. His gutteral speech—the sounds that a prelingually deaf person makes—sounded foreign to our ears, and in a nod to the ursine symbol of Russia, we called him "the bear that walks like a man." I actually did think on occasion that my father was a Russian spy and that if I woke him out of a deep sleep he'd betray himself by speaking Russian.

The game was fun, although underlying it was my unarticulated but deep sense that my father was foreign not only to the country but to me. He was faking some identity, and I could make him reveal it if I could only discover the right sneaky strategy. He was like Zorro's companion Bernardo, who pretended to be deaf so he could collect information for Zorro. No doubt we could make Dad confess that he could hear if we caught him by complete surprise.

When at last we had reached our target, after inching our way across the floor on our bellies unseen—we hoped—by our unsuspecting prey, we leapt up and pounced on him. Then we'd all wrestle in that animated way that fathers and sons use to express affection. In fact, my happiest times with my father were when we were wrestling. But I never got over the feeling that my father was someone I did not know, someone who could have been disguised as anything, someone with a secret that even he might not know.

IMPOTENT

Donor offspring . . . are constant reminders of their father's
inadequacy and failure. Men with low self-esteem and a shaky sense
of their masculinity are especially troubled by their offspring, who
have been genetically fathered by a virile specimen.

—ANNETTE BARAN AND REUBEN PANNOR, *LETHAL SECRETS:*
THE SHOCKING CONSEQUENCES AND PROBLEMS OF
ARTIFICIAL INSEMINATION

The husband may adapt himself badly to his adoptive fatherhood.
The constant presence of another's child may prove too irritating a
reminder to a man's sexual incompetence.

—WILFRED FINEGOLD, *ARTIFICIAL INSEMINATION*

My father is in the living room of our apartment in the Bronx. He
sits on a kitchen chair facing the black-and-white television console. The Emerson, encased in mahogany and trimmed in gold, is his
most valuable and prized possession. For us, living in a deaf environment, TV is a portal into the hearing world. But because my father
can't hear the shows he watches, and because closed captioning,
which allows deaf people to understand the audio portion of television programming, has not yet been invented, he remains outside
the hearing world, even when watching it. In fact, he turns off the
sound to save what he imagines to be the extra electricity used to

produce volume. So for him, watching TV involves a lot of complex visual decoding. When my brother or I watch, we of course keep the sound on, but then we have to explain the plots of shows to my father, a very annoying and distracting endeavor that we do without complaining, as just another of the many accommodations we are accustomed to making to our parents' deafness.

My grandfather, me, my father, and my brother—and the Emerson console

In our house, everything is geared toward being deaf. We live in a deaf world. We have a doorbell that "rings" by flashing a light and setting off a buzzer underneath my parents' pillows. We call each other by stamping our feet on the floor or rapping on the table to make vibrations, or by gesturing wildly to get the person's attention. Conversations are held with our fingers, and our faces are brilliant with the meaning of our signs, adding extra information. Outside is the hearing world with its abuses and its ignorance of our ways, its harsh, unfeeling regard for the deaf man or woman. The hearing world is full of flat, impassive faces, hands kept to the sides, eyes averted. Lips move without much revelation of their inner content. Faces remain immobile. But inside the house, all is deaf.

Within the dark living room—dark by virtue of facing the air shaft of the apartment building, what we romantically call the "court-yard"—my father sits confronting the screen that presents the hear-ing world in its black-and-white, fuzzy, soft-focus form. There are the blurry, jittery images of two men pummeling each other. Boxing. The two men are faceless as far as I am concerned, two hulks of hu-manity battling for some primordial principle. My father remains in his chair, but he is not still. In constant motion, he is shadowboxing. He takes every punch, throws a few. He is weaving and dodging, placing himself in defensive positions, then throwing his famous left hook. Watching television sports of any kind, be it baseball, boxing, or track and field, Morris is no longer an outsider. He's moving with the punches, cheering with the home runs, taking the curves on the Madison Square Garden running track. The cigar-smoking, incom-prehensibly chattering members of the audience don't matter; the artful dodge of the body and the heft of the muscles are all that count. With the sound turned off, the room is still, the only noise the high-pitched whine of the electrical tubes—like soprano cicadas on a summer's day. The roar of the crowd, the occasional *oof* from one of the men, the powerful thud of the punch—all are removed from the air. The only sounds are the ones my father makes. Each punch thrown on the screen evokes a muffled grunt from somewhere between his throat and his chest, like a cough combined with a moan. He's in the room, but in his mind my dad is the man in the silk boxer shorts weaving and bobbing—performing an exquisite dance in his chair that combines the pleasure of eluding attack and the thrill of lunging for the opponent.

My father during his youth in England had been a boxer. A handsome and athletic man in the second decade of the twentieth century, sporting a dapper moustache and sharp clothing, he had entered into the boxing ring along with other working-class Londoners, many Jewish, to duke it out before the eyes of the blood-thirsty audience. When he came home bruised and swollen-faced, his mother cried and begged him to stop boxing. But he was carrying on the family tradition. His father, Solomon Davis, had also been a boxer. Born in Kaunas (also known by the Polish name Kovno), Lithuania, in 1870, my grandfather had immigrated as a young man to London. There he became a fishmonger by trade but a boxer by avocation. A short, stocky man with a handlebar moustache, Solomon was a slow-footed pugilist with a single powerful defense—the left hook that was his secret weapon. So deadly was it that he once killed a man in the ring with a single punch. Those were the days when the gloves were off, literally.

Now in his fifties, my father sits at the television. Long gone are the unheard cheers and boos of the London ring. By now Morris has moved on to race-walking, the reigning passion of his life. But boxing remains a powerful metaphor for him. As he fights his shadow fight through the agency of the blurry men on the television set, he is having his day in court, protesting the injustice of being a Jewish deaf immigrant sweatshop worker. The court is the twelve-by-twelve-foot padded floor of the television boxing ring where the punches he throws are directed at the men who make his life hard and his feints and ducks help him dodge the slings and arrows of his difficult fortune. After each fight there remains the reality that he still has to go to work, toiling long days as a sewing machine operator in Manhattan's garment district. But while the fight is going on, the mimed play of offense and defense allows him to see himself as the boxer he once was, a man among his peers, a peer of his own realm, the vanquisher of foes.

To me, however, as a young child quietly observing him, there was something frightening about his almost epileptic absorption in the game. Yet even as I feared the strong and terrifying man with the violent temper who sat in the chair in the living room, his ferocity made me feel safe against attackers from outside. While in the drab reality of 1950s working-class New York he was but one of the drone-like minions who filed into factories with their lunch bags in their hands, I saw him as the ever-powerful father, the heroic vanquisher, the potent man with black hair on his body, a five o'clock shadow, and a manly moustache on his lip.

Was this protector my father? Was his potency enough to pluck the inchoate me from the chaos of the universe and brand me out for his own? Or was he an impotent man who knew that his sperm was weak, slow, and fallible? Was his shadowboxing a way to make him feel strong and to make me feel that he was the hypermasculine father that I seemed to need and that he seemed to want me to need? How would he have felt, then, if he had to ask his younger, more potent brother to stand in for him in the fertility arena, as my uncle claimed? Did it seem as if the referee and the crowds were laughing at him while he lay helpless on the floor, knocked down, the lights spinning around him with the confusion of the world itself? Or did he feel that he had feinted left and sailed out a powerful right punch when (and if) he tricked fate and got science and his brother to help him have a child? Was he the patsy or the con man? Did he win the match or was he the bleeding slumped thing on the canvas floor trying to regain consciousness and get to his feet as the referee counted in silent numbers the sum of his fate?

Never Say Die

My father could be a very determined man when he set his mind to it. Being deaf in those days cut him off from most avenues to professional success, but his determination found expression through amateur sports rather than his work. In the 1930s he held the American record for twenty-five miles in race-walking. The Ninety-second Street Young Men's Hebrew Association's trophy room was filled with my dad's trophies. I have a *New York Times* article from 1930 with the headline "50,000 Meter Walk Captured by Davis." The story goes on to say, "Morris Davis of the Ninety-second Street Y.M.H.A., a deaf mute, won his first major walking title, in leading home a field of twenty-eight starters . . . yesterday. Davis's time for the long grind, the distance of which is equivalent to 31 miles and 121 yards, was 5 hours and 26 minutes. A crowd of

My father, second from left (1925)

less than 100 persons, including the winner's father, himself a vet-eran walker, saw Davis cross the finish line."

I can envision Morris in his race-walking mode, his head held high and his long legs striding mightily, his lips set in a definite thin line of intent, no trace of humor on his visage. His eyes were always fixed ahead, even when I stood in the crowd waving. He never smiled as he passed me. He wasn't there for the admiration of the crowds or even that of his little son—he was there to win.

"Never say die" was a motto that buoyed my father, although in reality he had to say die to so many things. I can imagine that he might have drawn on this watchword phrase if he needed to fix the problem of his infertility. Another man might have given up and said die, but Morris might have determined to soldier on so that his wife could be happy with another child and his son could have a brother. Having lost his hearing, he might have regarded life as a race he needed to win, and winning might require extraordinary measures. When Morris was much older and succumbing to prostate cancer, I remember his repeatedly saying, his voice always filled with regret, as if he were in a race that he was finally losing, "You can't beat old age." He was so used to trying to beat things, pass his opponents on the racetrack, pummel them in the ring, defy the expectations of the hearing world, that the idea that there was something he couldn't beat seemed to strike him as a kind of sad novelty. But when he died, he did it quickly and with grace, rushing across this last finish line efficiently and with ease.

CLOSE EYES, SLEEP

Every night when I went to bed, my father would come in and bid me good night. I liked to be tucked in so tight that I was like a thin letter in a flat envelope. I guess I wanted to be swaddled against the dangers of the world, or mailed off to some secure destination in the land of Nod. I would insist that the covers be pulled tighter and tighter. How I could breathe at all was a wonder. Finally, when I'd made sure that I was cinched into bed with just the right amount of torque and that there was just enough but not too much light seeping in from the half-open door to remove the danger from the dark corners of the room, my father would say in his deep and guttural voice, always in the same order, "Good night. God bless. Close eyes. Sleep." The words came out not as a blessing but as a command. I was supposed to close my eyes and fall asleep immediately. No reading the way Abie did, no chitchat, no staring into the darkness, just a headlong rush into the arms of Morpheus.

My father would then leave, and I was expected to sleep. But I never did. I would lie in bed with my eyes wide open and alert to the dangers of the world. My brother, ten years older, was often out or away, and when he wasn't, he slept the sleep of a comatose adolescent. So I always felt alone, even with a brother. As the hypervigilant child of deaf parents, my role in life was to listen for the intruders, the fire alarms, the rumble of a tornado or earthquake. I developed elaborate compulsive rituals to keep myself from thinking of these dangers. I had to count the number of illuminated windows in the apartment building across the alleyway. This was an endless job, since upon finishing I'd always have to do a recount, on the possibility that someone had illuminated another room in the meantime. All of this obsessive activity was in the service of protecting my family and myself.

When my father would say his mantra to me each night, I think he felt he was protecting me. But, in reality, it was my job to protect him and my mother by listening, always listening.

My father intoned blessings all day long. He'd mutter prayers over food, upon leaving home, and at his return. And when he went to bed at night, he'd naturally say a protective blessing: "*Shma yisroel adonai elohanu adonai echod,*" hear O Israel, the Lord our God, the Lord is One.

Then he'd switch to English with "God bless" and a roll call of everyone in his family along with their place in the kinship system:

"Mother, father, sister Natalie, brother Abie, wife Eva, son Gerald, and"—always a fraction-of-a-second pause—"son Lenny." I was always last. And I wondered always if I was also least.

After he blessed me, he would utter the same command to himself that he said to me each night: "Close eyes. Sleep."

Maybe it worked for him, but it never worked for me. In that family, no one was brave enough to admit that you can't just say "Close eyes, sleep" and expect anything with a mammalian nervous system to drop off to sleep. Did my father really expect me to go to sleep at his command? Did I really think I should? I don't recall ever saying to him, "Hey, Dad, you know, I never fall asleep when you do that. In fact, I stay up for a long time worrying about things, especially about dying. I worry about fires, and thieves, and various other terrifying things. I lie here protecting us all."

He wouldn't have gotten my point because in our family there was a belief that with the right kind of effort the human mind could be brought under control. If you had to go to sleep, you could be told to do so by a sufficiently powerful father, and you would. Emotions or worries that might keep you awake were simply wrong and could be eliminated by intoning the correct formula. "Good night. God bless. Close eyes. Sleep" was the formula of choice. Like many of my father's bromides, this one clearly worked for him and so it stood to reason in his tidy brain that it would work for me.

But it didn't. And it probably didn't really work for him, either—no matter how he may have tried to make it work. I would never know because in our family our feelings and failings were kept to ourselves.

BETTER NOT TO KNOW

Some things were best left unsaid. If you couldn't command reality, then you could at least forget about it.

My mother often talked to her friends about "women's problems." What were they? I'd always ask. Better not to know.

What about death? I'd ask my mother endless questions about dying, but she would just say it was better not to know. When my great-aunt Jeanne died, I asked what she died of. The answer was "old age." But I wanted to know more. How did you die of old age? Wasn't there a particular cause? Better not to know.

How much money did my parents earn? They'd never say.

How old was my mother? "Twenty-one plus" was her unchanging answer. I assume she developed that one because she was, to use her term, "an old maid" when she finally married at twenty-seven. But I'd always want to know. Like Oedipus, I couldn't leave well enough alone.

How did you have sex? There was no answer for me. Better not to know, so I looked in my brother's biology textbooks and read books with titles like *Facts of Life and Love for Teen-agers*.

If my uncle's story is correct, I wonder if my parents stopped consciously thinking or talking about my origin. I wonder if they were able to put this secret into the better-not-to-know box, seal it up, and throw it into some sluggish, muddy river of mental oblivion.

As I grew up I adopted my parents' don't-ask-don't-tell policy and used it to keep them at arm's length. They knew almost nothing about me. Morris and Eva lived in their deaf world, and I lived sometimes in their world and sometimes in the hearing world. I went to college and left their working-class background behind. They couldn't understand what I studied, and I didn't care much about what they did. Only later in life did I start to study deafness and realize the rich complexity of the world I had left. But the family lesson had left its mark: better not to know, especially better not to know or reveal oneself.

GOOD FATHER, GOOD SON

My father was fond of saying "Good father, good son" as another kind of protective mantra. I think he used the phrase to protect himself against being a bad father and me from being the bad son. Being a bad son might have meant being the son I already secretly was. Or maybe it meant being like Abie.

I remember being an angsty adolescent and having a major fight with Morris. I told him that I had had a miserable and unhappy childhood, upping the hyperbole at the urging of teen hormones. My father looked at me uncomprehendingly and said, "No, you had a happy childhood. Good father, good son." I probably threw myself on the floor and cried in frustration or stormed out of the room. But the power of positive thinking inherent in my father's phrase guaranteed for him that he was, had to be, of course would have been, a good father. And I, by contract or by concession, would of course be a good son. But if he was not my biological father, as Abie had insinuated, how much of this was Morris trying to prop himself up? If his sperm hadn't been the life-giver, he could at least comfort himself that he had been a good father. Likewise, if I was Abie's son, the mantra would ensure that I would steer clear of the bad-seed influences of Morris's younger and problematic brother and learn by nurture, if not by nature, how to be the good son of the good father.

Don't Get Excited;
You'll Only Be Disappointed

My father had a lot of these expressions, but the key one my mother often used with me was "Don't get excited; you'll only be disappointed." My mother had low expectations. As a working-class woman, she easily accommodated herself to the wrongs of life. And in her case, the wrongs included her early deafness. She didn't expect much from life, and she was if not satisfied, at least resigned to the modesty of whatever material objects and emotional rewards she and my father had managed to accrue. The goal was to aim low and avoid the risks of aspiring to higher achievements.

I was, as all children are, enthusiastic. I loved life and wanted to see everything and do everything. I was naturally excited about a trip to the zoo or an upcoming birthday. Even an ice cream on a hot summer afternoon was worthy of a few jumps up and down and some verbal crowing. The job of my mother was to tamp down my enthusiasm. She'd been through the school of hard knocks and had been one of its best students. Coming close to dying in early childhood, surviving meningitis but losing her hearing, being sent away from her parents to deaf school, living the life of a shop girl in England and then a factory worker in the United States, she was summa cum laude in the college of disappointments. Now her job was to mentor the new student in life—that would have been me.

My father (left), Gerald (right), and me (center)

What is amazing to me is that if what Abie said to me was true, it would seem that when faced with what would surely have been one of her greatest disappointments, that of her husband's infertility, her constitutional downward tilt toward low expectations suddenly shifted upward. She knew how to make the best of a bad situation. Perhaps this one time, deciding to go to the gynecologist for artificial insemination, she did get her hopes up. Another way of looking at it is that she didn't get her hopes up at all: she simply resigned herself to the only possible way out of the infertility dilemma. In any case, she must have wanted a second child so much that she was willing to overcome her natural tendency toward stasis and resignation in order to right what must have seemed like a cosmic injustice.

Looking back, I see how easy it is to hear the keywords of my childhood as substitutes for the words my parents might not have been able to bring themselves to say—and to understand them as clues to the big secret of my existence.

FOUR

Artificial Bastards and Ghost Fathers

IN 1949, THE YEAR I WAS BORN, donor insemination was still very controversial. Three days after my birth, the *New York Times* carried a story about Catholic doctors who had met to condemn the process as illegal and immoral. Publications such as the *New York Times* and *Newsweek* decried "ghost fathers" and "synthetic babies." The science and technology of assisted reproduction had come a long way by then, but the moral issues still resonated, and they found expression in the law.

In America, several states proposed legislation to ban donor insemination, some of which was passed into law. A number of states (and religions) considered the married woman who underwent artificial insemination to be an adulteress and the resulting child to be illegitimate. The father and the supervising doctor were considered guilty of conspiracy to commit adultery as well as fraud, since by signing the birth certificate swearing that the man was the father of the child he did not sire, both the father and the doctor were acting illegally. The courts set the standard in these cases. One legal dispute involving a Chicago couple in 1954 was resolved with the judge's ruling that donor insemination, with or without consent, was immoral, that the wife was an adulteress, and that the child was a bastard. Even the *Journal of the American Medical Association* and the Legal Bureau of the AMA came out against donor insemination, citing various legal decisions and statutes that not only made the offspring of artificial insemination illegitimate but also precluded them from inheriting property, even if formally adopted. In the late 1950s the Federal Republic of Germany and Italy entertained bills put before their parliaments that would have made donor insemination a criminal offense.

The moral and legal ramifications of artificial and most particularly donor insemination were hotly debated in many other countries, too. Going back to 1921, the supreme court of Ontario had ruled that donor insemination constituted adultery in the test tube. Some critics called donor offspring "artificial bastards," and a *Time* magazine article in 1945 had the headline "Artificial Bastards?" In 1948, the archbishop of Canterbury issued a report conducted by a wide variety of legal, religious, and ethical experts that condemned the procedure. The archbishop acknowledged that artificial insemination might improve a marriage, but the report considered it analogous to adultery, saying that just as having an affair to preserve a marriage might make sense to a husband or a wife, "they would hardly do so on the ground that Christian marriage was what they contended for, and wished to maintain," so, too, with donor insemination.

In England around the time of my birth, Dr. Mary Barton and her husband, Bertold Wiesner—a scientist who did some of the early research on sex hormones—published an article advocating donor insemination in the *British Medical Journal* that provoked an uproar in Parliament. Lord Bothwall called the practice "vile," adding that "Mary Barton seems to forget that men are not cattle." The newspaper article describing Lord Bothwall's protest added that "many Lords seemed to regard that the procedure is not only a threat to the British family and morals but also brings into question the legitimacy of titles." Another British newspaper of the period ran a headline "Artificial Insemination: Is It Right or Wrong?" The article goes on to say that "more than nine out of ten of our readers say it is WRONG. But the scientists insist on carrying on."

Aside from the legal, moral, and societal issues, the processes involved in collecting semen and inseminating women were themselves wrapped in controversy. Since most semen was obtained from masturbation (resulting in what physicians euphemistically and clinically called a "friction specimen"), the very act of producing it was considered at the time to be sinful by some religions, notably the Catholic and Anglican churches, as well as unhealthy according to various medical and psychological experts ranging from Freud to Havelock Ellis. As one British writer put it, "to most balanced men the task of donation is unpleasant." Another wrote, "When, as is usual, the semen is obtained by masturbation, the possibility of untoward psychological consequences arising from this cause alone must be reckoned with." While we joke about masturbation today and see it as a normal and self-actuating activity, merely fifty years ago it was still considered unsavory and damaging to one's health and mental well-being. Some proponents of artificial insemination developed quite painful and invasive techniques for the removal of sperm without masturbation to avoid the stigma.

The issue of individual donors fathering legions of children they would never know also raised serious moral questions, with some donors reported to have sired hundreds, even thousands, of offspring. In England, Barton and Wiesner established a clinic and recruited an elite band of respectable, married, high-IQ donors to provide sperm for artificial insemination. Among them was the brilliant neuroscientist Derek Richter, who was selected because of his enormous intellect and whose semen purportedly sired more than a hundred children by 1948. In addition to Richter, it seems that many scientists and doctors, including perhaps J.B.S. Haldane, Julian Huxley, and others, might have given their semen. Having discovered that only a very small amount of semen was necessary for fertilization—"a fecund donor submitting two specimens weekly could, with ideal conditions, produce 400 children weekly (that is, 20,000 annually)"—Barton and Wiesner set an "arbitrary limit of 100 children for each donor." The results of this prolific donor insemination program are only now in the process of being discovered, as a growing number of the offspring of these supposed geniuses are tracing their origins to the Barton-Wiesner clinic. Canadian filmmaker Barry Stevens has made a film called *Offspring* recounting his and his sister Janice Stevens Botsford's attempt to find their siblings, all of whom came from Barton and Wiesner's clinic. At latest count, Stevens estimates that he has upward of five hundred siblings and Janice about two hundred. The discoveries that some of these offspring have made about their half siblings have given rise to quite a number of unconventional family units, as the newfound blood relatives decide to embrace one another. This primal feeling for family is cropping up in many different contexts. One such story that has arisen, covered by CBS News, is that of two California women who met at a party and discovered that their children were conceived through donor insemination at the same San Diego clinic. When they compared notes about the anonymous donor, they realized that donor 48QAH was the common father of both children. Now they are raising their children as siblings. Such experiments as these raise questions about the very nature of the nuclear family.

In small towns and cities where multiple inseminations from one donor occurred, there were potentially serious health and perhaps moral issues raised because of the statistically significant chance that those children might meet and marry without realizing that they were brother and sister. In one case, a doctor in a small town had artificially inseminated a number of women, many of whose offspring sprouted the signature red hair of the doctor.

With talk of donor insemination as a form of adultery, there was a certain sexual frisson about the process. There was even a British movie made in 1959 about donor insemination called *A Question of Adultery*. The film starred the sexy, sultry American singer Julie London, whose hits included "Makin' Whoopee" and the very suggestive "Go Slow." London played a woman who is problematically married to a hot-tempered race car driver with a jealous streak. She becomes pregnant, hoping that the baby will bring harmony back to their discordant relationship and save their marriage. When the two get into a terrible auto accident, she loses the baby and her husband is rendered infertile. She then opts for donor insemination, to which her husband reluctantly consents. But after she gets pregnant from the procedure, he has second thoughts and changes his mind. The couple breaks up, and he sues for divorce on the grounds of adultery. At one point in the movie, the husband's testy, bewigged attorney chastises the medical doctor who performed the insemination: "At that rate any woman who commits adultery can deny it, saying, 'It was by artificial insemination.' Ask Dr. Cameron, who conjures up these phantom fathers to fill the world with test tube babies!" In the end, the jury is unable to decide the case, but the couple reconciles, the husband goes on to become a wonderful father, and the sanctity of the nuclear family, even if donor-created, is upheld.

Even as late as 1989, in a book titled *Lethal Secrets: The Shocking Consequences and Unsolved Problems of Artificial Insemination* by Annette Baran and Reuben Pannor, we find an account of the pseudonymous "Carly" daydreaming and fantasizing about the donor as she prepares herself to receive his sperm:

> Her usual evening ablutions seemed to take on a special significance, and she added a few extra routines usually reserved for special evenings out. Like she was single again, going on an exciting date?
>
> "What a nut I am!" she giggled. As she lay back in the tub, she found herself thinking about the man whose sperm she would receive. She knew that he was a student at the university medical school, and that he was healthy, young and nice-looking.... Carly tried to imagine what the donor would look like....
>
> Carly sank farther down into the warm water and continued with her fantasy....She put him in a small room with a cot, a chair, some magazines, girlie magazines, and a small adjoining toilet....Now came the important part. Carly shook her head;

she realized that she had never seen a male masturbate. She knew that they did and she knew that that was how her donor's sperm would get into the wide-necked bottle. She knew too that she had fantasized about various men making love to her, but never about masturbating. The scene became disturbing, and then exciting, and then disturbing again; finally he ejaculated into the bottle.

These accounts reveal the potentially eroticized aspect of donor insemination, as well as the drama of it, in the fantasy lives of married women. On the other hand, there was the "ick" factor of receiving a total stranger's bodily fluid, not to mention the health hazard. In the early days of insemination, it was entirely possible that semen could be contaminated with germs that might transmit venereal disease. Not surprisingly, in vitro fertilization, in which an egg is fertilized outside the womb and the resulting embryo is then implanted, quickly became the preferred method for infertile couples as soon as it was introduced in the 1960s, and it has remained such.

Because of the shame, legal complications, and general societal disapproval associated with donor insemination, there was until relatively recently an entire culture of secrecy surrounding it. Husbands, wives, physicians, and donors were all equally sworn to maintain that secrecy. Medical books on artificial insemination suggested that doctors arrange to have donors hand off their specimens to couriers, leaving the donor in the dark about where his gametes might be heading. Parents were warned never to reveal the truth to their children, grandparents, other relatives, or friends, because if they ever did let the secret out, the results would be "devastating." So the whole process was like a spy drama or a bank heist, with all parties guilty and sworn to secrecy. However, the result of all this secrecy was that children who were conceived under such circumstances often—perhaps inevitably—picked up on the sense of some kind of a lurking secret surrounding the circumstances of their birth.

Recent psychological studies exploring the actual effects of such secrecy have discovered that it has a much more devastating result than might full disclosure. Fathers who have to keep their infertility secret and pretend to be potent suffer considerable mental stress. The man who labors under this kind of secrecy is put in a difficult position. He will have to lie to the world and proclaim himself the proud dad. He'll hand out cigars, pretending his masculinity led to the happy event. When the child is born, he will scour its face to discern the identity of the man who is actually the biological father. Inevitably he will find in the child faults and disappointments, or perhaps abilities and talents, that he will see as alien and even threatening. Mothers who were fulfilled in their childbearing desires by a man other than their husband must process the resulting ambivalence toward both their husband and their child, and so must the husband, whose sense of jealousy and inferiority might wreak havoc on a marital relationship—to say nothing of how the child is affected. A consistent theme in the testimony of donor offspring is that they "knew" something was wrong. Many recount being treated oddly by their fathers. One notes, "I never had a father who felt like he was my father."

There are medical as well as psychological ramifications to donor insemination. In one case, five children fathered by the same sperm donor developed a rare genetic disease. Although donors are routinely tested to see if they have alleles for common genetic diseases such as cystic fibrosis and Tay-Sachs, they aren't tested for rarer, more unusual diseases. Since this case involves a donor who requested anonymity, and since the sperm bank must honor the confidentiality of the process, it will not contact the donor to inform him that he carries the genes for neutrophilia, a disease of the white blood cells that appears in one in five million children. Further, since there is no communication between sperm banks, if the donor sells his sperm to any of the other companies that provide this service, there is no way of preventing him from continuing to spread the genes for this rare disease.

And then there are the aesthetic problems with artificial insemination. What's the difference between having sex and being artificially inseminated? For some the difference may seem largely a matter of taste. In the first case, there might under ideal circumstances be romance, candlelight, a dinner in which the man and woman gaze into each other's eyes, drink a few glasses of wine, and end up in bed, locked in each other's loving embrace, knowing that their lovemaking has the potential to produce both passion and a child. In the case of artificial insemination, it's harder to be romantic. Candles will be replaced by fluorescent lights. The romantic setting will give way to the doctor's office or clinic. The rush of sexual tension will be forgotten as a vial of sperm and a syringe are clinically inserted into the cervix. The elements of impulsivity and serendipity will give way to the planned, controlled act of insemination. And almost always, the donor will be unknown, except for a code number.

Donor insemination has become big business in the United States and worldwide. An estimated thirty thousand children are conceived each year in this way. By now upward of a million children have been born by donor insemination—enough to fill a small city. Nowadays it's possible and easy to perform an in-home donor insemination. Online catalogues of potential donors abound. Women, married or single, heterosexual or lesbian, can read the specs describing potential fathers, including their physical attributes, mental abilities, and likes and dislikes. These Web sites resemble nothing so much as dating services. Once a woman has decided on her future inseminator, she can give a credit card number and receive by FedEx a refrigerated sample of sperm for use in the privacy of her home.

The journey from forbidden practice to consumer activity has taken about a hundred years, and what before was a moral calamity to most people is now a relatively well-accepted alternative. The moral and legal issues seem to have all but disappeared (though the Roman Catholic Church still disapproves). Many states now have laws expressly legitimizing the social father rather than the biological one as the legal parent.

Yet most of the children born by this method still share one core issue: they don't know their biological fathers. Now many sperm banks allow a grown child to locate his or her donor if the donor agrees to such a request. As the culture of secrecy shifts and more and more donors become willing to be identified, some of the most troubling aspects of artificial insemination related to secrets and lies will go by the wayside. There is an active movement spearheaded by donor offspring who are trying to pass laws that would completely do away with secrecy. England is on the verge of passing a new law requiring that donor information be included on the national birth certificate. And as of 2005, donor anonymity has been abolished in the U.K.

But donor insemination will never be just a simple medical procedure. It will always carry the complexity of a practice that results in children fathered out of wedlock, the mixed feelings engendered by questions of origin. And those mixed feelings are as true for me as they are for everyone else who has ever had to wonder about his or her parentage.

FIVE

Looking for Answers

I WROTE MY MEMOIR *MY SENSE OF SILENCE* in the 1990s, and in it I recounted my life story from birth until my twenty-second year, the year my mother died. I wrote about almost everything that seemed of interest about myself and my family, but I didn't tell the story of Abie's phone call, because I didn't feel comfortable repeating it. What if what he said wasn't true at all? I didn't want to give it credit if credit wasn't due. Besides, at that point, the very idea that my uncle may have been my father was so deeply disturbing to me that I barely wanted to tell myself the story, let alone share it with the public. I told only my wife and one close friend. I didn't even tell my brother.

Time provided a certain insulation if not comfort. Being well trained in "better not to know," I moved from my thirties to my fifties managing to block most of the emotion connected with the information. Whenever the notion that Morris was not my father would surface, I would bury it, as I had buried him. But there also grew in me a gnawing curiosity, the beginning of an obsession.

Could my uncle's story possibly be true? Or was it a fantasy on his part? So much of it made sense, but so much else was murky. And Abie was so unstable and unreliable it was hard to believe anything he said.

In 2004, I decided to find out what I could, and to tell my story—whatever it was—in book form, taking it public. Slowly over the years I had begun writing more and more self-revealing articles. I began to realize that keeping things secret gave them a negative power of their own. I recalled a line from the poet Rilke that said something like "Nakedness is my armor." It's true that when you are naked you have nothing more to hide. The same is true of writing. By writing these words right now, I am in a process of freeing myself from particular kinds of guilt and shame. And by including readers in my feelings and thoughts through the act of making the process public, I have a sense of not being alone, even though as I write this very sentence I am sitting by myself in a silent room.

To investigate Abie's claim of paternity, I called a few genetic testing labs I'd found on the Internet. The people at the labs told me it would be very difficult to sort through the family DNA without actual genetic material from my father, mother, and Abie. But all of those key players in my story were dead and had been for a fairly long time. The problem was compounded by the fact that since Abie and Morris were brothers, they shared the same DNA on the Y chromosome, the chromosome that passes down from father to son relatively unchanged, so if I was the offspring of either Morris or Abie, looking for current male members of the Davis clan and comparing them with me would yield little if any information. We'd all have the same Y chromosome.

So I remained stumped, and the investigation seemed permanently stalled. Then that fall I went to a conference at Duke University on genetics and culture. One of the keynote speakers was Dr. Wayne Grody of the UCLA Medical Center. Wayne Grody was an unassuming-looking man in his early fifties at the time. He was one of the keynoters at the conference, and he gave a delightful talk with lots of PowerPoint help that wasn't exactly about the subject of the conference but more about how he had come to be interested in being a doctor and then in genetics. His youth had involved reading the same comics and watching the same TV shows as I had. He showed us photos of the covers of books that influenced his desire to be a doctor when he was a young boy in the fifties, as well as stills from television shows about physicians such as *Dr. Kildare* and *Ben Casey*. (He identified with the former more than the latter, and I had always felt that way, too.) He recounted how he became interested in genetics and eventually became the head of the Genetics Lab at UCLA. Along the way, he started writing a column for a medical journal in which he reviewed films. That work led to his being contacted by Hollywood studios to serve as a consultant on films and TV shows that dealt with genetics. He had worked on films such as *ET* and *Outbreak* as well as *The X-Files*.

Partly because Wayne was about my age and had grown up in a Jewish family on the East Coast, I felt an instant bond with him. After his talk, I approached him and told him my story. He was more than willing to help, but of course faced the same problem that any other researcher would: I had no DNA from Morris or Abie. Wayne thought a bit, and then the proverbial lightbulb appeared over his head.

"Why don't you try to find a paraffin block?"

"What's that?" I asked.

"Well, whenever anyone goes to a hospital for surgery or a biopsy, or whenever someone dies in a hospital or other institution, they usually take a bit of tissue and store it in paraffin."

"Paraffin! Like candle wax?"

"Yes, exactly. So if your father or Abie was ever in a hospital, there should be a bit of their bodies encased in paraffin that you could locate. If the sample was in good shape, we could get enough DNA off it to run a test."

Now things were taking a Madame Tussaud's turn. My long-dead father and uncle were preserved in wax! I thought about the last ten years of my father's life, during which he had been treated for cancer of the prostate. He'd been in and out of hospitals over that period. After a biopsy at Beth Israel in New York revealed the cancer, he was operated on and had part of his prostate removed. When the cancer returned, he had an orchidectomy, an operation in which the testicles are removed to eliminate testosterone, which can accelerate the growth of prostate cancer. That treatment worked for a few years, but eventually he had to return to the hospital for radiological treatment of metastases to the spine, followed by treatment for acute renal failure. He spent his last days in a nursing home. So there were a number of occasions when tissue taken from his body could have been preserved in the way that Wayne was describing. I was suddenly back on track, if only I could locate and obtain this material.

I thanked Wayne, and we agreed that we'd talk again when and if I located a paraffin block with my father's tissues.

Trying to dig up a piece of the dead isn't easy these days. Stricter laws now make it almost impossible to get hold of a patient's medical records, even if the person is dead and he's your father. The general idea is that your medical history is your own, and no one has a right to see it other than those you choose. Even if you are dead, you still have rights.

I started making phone calls to Beth Israel Hospital, where I encountered the Kafkaesque bureaucracy that haunts all such large institutions. I managed to get to the records bureau, but they couldn't or wouldn't locate Morris's records. I was prepared for a similar runaround at Columbia University Medical Center, but, surprisingly, I was able to find my way to the pathology lab, where I spoke to an administrator named Maria who said she would investigate. I wasn't expecting much.

I called back a few times and got only her answering machine. Then one day I picked up the phone and was surprised to hear Maria on the other end of the line.

"Dr. Davis?" she asked. (I often preface the honorific "Dr." to my name when dealing with hospital staff. It does wonders, and I *am* a doctor, of course, but of literature, not medicine. Now I am also a member of the Department of Medical Education, which gets me even closer to what they think I might be.)

"Yes?"

"It's Maria at Columbia. We've located the records for your father. And there appears to be a paraffin block that we have in storage."

I couldn't believe that there could actually be a trace of my father still in existence more than twenty years after his death.

"Are you sure this is the same Morris Davis?"

"Yes."

"From Nagel Avenue?"

"Yes, Dr. Davis. But you can't get access to the sample unless you have power of attorney."

A catch! I had to call my brother, Gerald, and ask him whether he had been given power of attorney. When my father died I was fairly oblivious to the legal proceedings, but my brother, ten years older and probably more involved in them than I, might remember. He had subsequently been an insurance salesman and had some experience dealing with estates.

I hadn't told my brother about any of the story concerning Abie, so now I would have to reveal to him not only what Abie had told me but also why I had never said anything about it for so many years. My brother and I had only recently begun to be closer after a long period of relative distance. There was never a dispute that kept us apart. It was more just a difference of personalities. I'd always wanted him to be more open emotionally. He tended toward being controlled and formal. Our British parents didn't go in for displays of emotion, and my brother, the firstborn, picked up a good deal of their way of being in the world. And then there were my memories of the past. Gerald liked tormenting me when I was a child, often teasing me verbally and roughing me up physically so I'd end up in tears. He must have learned this from my father, who seemed to enjoy taunting us—especially me, perhaps because I was known as the "sensitive" one in the family. Because of this history, Gerald was the last person at that time I would have considered confiding in, allowing him to see my vulnerability. Now I'd be telling my brother something that made me extremely uncomfortable, and I could only hope that he wouldn't laugh a hurtful laugh and dismiss me or, worse, privately exult that he was the only true son of our father. I wasn't sure that Gerald had the emotional tact to make me feel okay about sharing this intimacy with him. Over the years, I had gone through a lot of therapy, and he had gone through none. So we didn't talk the same emotional language. And then there was, of course, the universal and enduring issue of sibling rivalry.

But if I wanted to get access to the paraffin block, I was going to have to tell Gerald why, to let him know that I thought I might not be our father's son. I assumed that Gerald's own paternity was not in question, for there was nothing to suggest that he was the product of donor insemination. My parents were married in September 1938 and Gerald was born in October 1939, when Morris was forty-one. It might have been that Morris's low sperm count, the result of an adolescent bout with mumps, perhaps compounded by the damage caused by a gonorrheal infection, had allowed him to function well enough to father one child in his forties, but had then deteriorated so much in subsequent years that he was left completely infertile—that is, if Abie's story were true.

Since my brother and I have perfected a virtual script for our telephone calls, I knew I could begin this momentous conversation with our standard routine. We always cover how our family members are, talk about films we've seen, books we've read. So when I called Gerald we began with the usual fare. But I was nervous about the revelation I'd have to make. Gerald was, of course, oblivious to the fact that I was going to change our script.

"Listen, I have to tell you something."

"What?"

"I never told you this, and I hope you won't be angry, but when Dad died I got a phone call from Abie."

"Yes?"

"And he told me..." I almost couldn't get the words out. "That he thought he was my father."

There was a long silence on the other end.

"That's ridiculous!" was all Gerald said.

"Well, it isn't what you think."

"Mom would never have..." He trailed off indignantly.

"No, it's that he claimed to have been my donor for artificial insemination."

"I don't believe a word of it. Did they even have artificial insemination back then?" Although his tone was detached and remote, I could sense his discomfort. "Anyway, Abie was not to be trusted. I wouldn't believe anything he told you."

"I didn't," I said, "at first. But I did some research and a lot of what he said turns out to be true. There was artificial insemination at the time; they did often ask brothers to contribute; and, just as he told me, they did make a practice of mixing the semen of the donor and the infertile father."

"They mixed the semen? Well, then even if what he says is true..." He was searching in his mind for a way to make the situation go away.

"Well, to be sure, I'm going to do DNA testing, and I need to know if we have power of attorney."

"I'm sure whatever Abie said was not true. You're my brother and that's it." I appreciated his wanting the bond between us to be kept intact, but I felt that his dismissal of my concerns was too pat and too quick. Once again I was being the "sensitive" one, not letting things slide, not letting well enough alone.

When I persisted, Gerald agreed to look into the question of power of attorney. A week later he called back.

"It turns out that I do have power of attorney." Suddenly it struck me as strange that only he would have been given power of attorney. I began to get a bit paranoid. Had Morris not considered me to be his full son? Now I remembered that when he decided to give us some of his savings in advance of his death, he gave Gerald far more than he gave me. At the time he said Gerald needed the money more because he was married. But why wouldn't I need it when I got married? And when I did, I never got the balance to right the inequity.

"Good, now I can get the sample."

"I really don't think you need to do this. It's a waste of time and obviously not true."

"Yeah, but I need to know."

"Why? What difference would it make? I'm your brother. Morris was your father—he raised you. Why do you need to know?"

"I'm not sure, but it does make a difference. And if it were true, you would only be my half brother."

There was a silence as this fact sank in.

"Wouldn't make a difference to me." But I could detect what my brother couldn't: it would make a difference. It would have to.

"Even if it was true, Abie shouldn't have told you. He broke a promise. It was ungentlemanly," Gerald went on.

"But it was a pretty big secret. Could you keep that all your life?"

"He was supposed to."

"Well, I'd rather know."

"It's better not to know something like this."

Better not to know. This familiar advice took me back to the events surrounding my mother's death. I was twenty-two at the time and living in Paris, where I was doing graduate studies toward my Ph.D. I received a telegram from my brother, telling me that our mother had been hit by a truck and suffered a ruptured spleen. When she arrived at the hospital she was pronounced DOA, but was then revived and hooked up to machines that were keeping her alive. Gerald told me to get back to New York as soon as I could.

Without a ticket, I headed to the airport, and had a harrowing time finding a seat on a plane to the United States. Only by the sheerest act of will did I make it back to New York City that same day. After the usual chaos at JFK airport, I took a taxi to my brother's apartment, where I found my brother and father walking the corridor outside the elevator, their faces masks of grief. Mother was still alive, but in an irreversible coma, they told me. I wanted to see her immediately. But my father and brother said, "Better not to see her. Just remember her as she was." They were afraid she was disfigured, crushed and unrecognizable from the impact of the truck. Both of them had been to the hospital and talked to the doctors, but although twenty-four hours had now passed, neither had gone into her room. Better not to know.

We took a taxi in silence to the hospital. On arriving we met the supervising physician. He told us that she was "brain-dead" and

My mother

that she'd be disconnected from the life support equipment after forty-eight hours of zero EKG. Everything in me wanted to go to my mother. I wanted desperately to see her, hold her hand, stroke her hair. She was my mother, and I loved her. She had been my childhood companion, the only one in the family who cherished me, who loved me simply and without ambivalence or complication. Morris and Gerald told me again, "Better not to see her. Remember her the way she was." But I couldn't do that. I pushed my way through the double doors of the hallway leading to her room and headed in what I thought was the right direction. When I looked into what I believed was her room, however, she wasn't there. It was the wrong room. I went from room to room but couldn't find her. And at each room I could hear my father's and my brother's words echoing in my brain: *Better not to see her. Remember her.* A dread entered my being. At twenty-two, I didn't have the inner strength to keep looking. Deferring to my elders, I went back to the waiting room to join my "not knowing" family. She was dead the next day.

Even to this moment, I regret so much losing my courage, not sticking with my original instinct. This is one of the great misgivings of my life. Even though I know she was not conscious and wouldn't have known I was there, some part of me feels as if she would have. It would have been better to know. As it was, she died alone.

But the story doesn't end there. The day she died we got a phone call from the coroner's office. Since this was a homicide, a hit-and-run crime, we'd have to identify her at the morgue. The little defensive strategy my family had employed to avoid seeing her was no longer operative. My father couldn't bring himself to transgress the don't-look-don't-tell rule. My brother was unwilling to go alone, and so was I. So Gerald and I ended up going to the morgue together. When we got there, we first had to sign a sheaf of papers. Then we were led down a nondescript hallway and told to wait at the head of a flight of dingy concrete steps. At a signal we were to walk, one at a time, down the steps, glance to our left through a door, and then quickly exit to our right. We both memorized these instructions, which had no doubt proved effective over the course of many years of dealing with distraught family members.

My brother went first. I watched him walk down the steps with dread, cast his eyes quickly to the left, bend over, collapse into tears, and immediately turn to his right and walk away. The whole tightly choreographed scene took five seconds.

Now it was my turn. I walked down the steps, preparing myself to see a mangled, disfigured corpse. I turned my head to the left and saw not some hideous thing but my own lovely, sweet mother. She was lying on her back, looking beautiful, her nose a bit more prominent in death, and her hair pulled back in an unaccustomed manner by some hasty morgue attendant. I turned and started to walk away, imitating my brother, but then stopped, turned, went back, and just gazed on her for several minutes. My last look. It was the saddest moment in my life up to that point, and possibly ever. I wanted to stay there and not let her or the moment go. Finally I turned and left.

For my brother, the viewing was a horror. It confirmed his dictum: better not to know. For me the opportunity to have that moment with my mother was a blessing, confirming my own credo: knowing is all there is. The same feelings were motivating me now. I felt I had to press on to find out if Morris was my father. It was as though I were Oedipus, intent on discovering a familial secret about my origins, a truth that no one wanted me to find out. Someone had whispered in my ear that my father wasn't my father, and now I was heading for the DNA oracle to find out the truth. But as with Oedipus, perhaps this passion for discovering family secrets and for revealing what has been long buried was a form of recklessness. I had doubts about whether to proceed, but the quest had now become an obsession, and I felt there was no turning back.

I called Maria and told her that my brother did have power of attorney. She told me she'd retrieve the paraffin block. Then I waited.

Several weeks passed, and I began mechanically to telephone Maria each day with no result. Finally, one day, she phoned me.

"Dr. Davis, we have the sample here."

"You do?"

"Yes. We can't send you the entire thing, but we can cut it into slices and send those. Where shall we send them?"

"Are you sure this sample is from Morris Davis?"

She reassured me once again.

"Right address?"

Yes, correct address.

Now I needed to contact Wayne Grody at UCLA. I called him and he gave me the instructions for sending the materials to him, what size slices and how many he needed. And I had to send a sample of my blood to him as well. I had thought a cheek swab would suffice, but Wayne said blood would be better and more accurate.

I filled out many forms, and my brother provided the necessary power of attorney. The bits of my father were sliced up and sent by FedEx to Wayne. But strangely enough, getting my own blood sample to him proved a bit more problematic than I expected. I didn't have a prescription for the blood draw and my doctor's office wouldn't send it through the mail, only to their own laboratories. In fact, no hospital or doctor I could find would draw the blood and send it overnight to UCLA. Their procedures were all geared to sending blood to labs for analysis. And individuals can't send blood through the mail; only doctors and labs can.

The clock was ticking and I couldn't figure out what to do.

Then I remembered that I had a friend whose son and daughter-in-law were medical residents at a local New York hospital. I called them and, after explaining the situation, asked if they would draw the blood, which I would then FedEx myself to Wayne. They agreed, and we made arrangements for me to come to them after they got off work. They lived in Harlem, so I soon found myself driving to Harlem at 10:00 P.M. to get my blood taken. I parked my car in a somewhat dodgy neighborhood and rang the doorbell to Anna and Jacob's brownstone apartment. Jacob spoke through the intercom and rang me in. I climbed the flights of stairs and was greeted by the young couple, who were cooking a late-night dinner. They discussed who was better at taking blood, and decided that Anna should do it. And there in their kitchen, they laid out the materials and pierced my vein. It felt like I was having an illicit moment in Harlem, not unlike the many other folks who were no doubt opening their veins at that very moment to shoot up. Once the vial of red blood was handed to me, I absconded with it, vanishing into the night, feeling criminal all around—for taking blood in this illicit way, for trying to find out something that was kept secret, for being the possible test tube bastard that artificial insemination had produced. I wondered if Morris had had any such sensations when—and if—he carried Abie's semen from Fourteenth Street to the Upper West Side to fertilize my mother.

Once everything had been sent, I waited.

I began to wonder how I wanted this to come out. Did I want Abie or Morris as my father? Frankly, some part of me wanted neither. And yet I did want Morris so that I could preserve the comfortably familiar architecture of my whole history. I didn't want to pull out the capstone of the arch of my life and have it fall in on me. I wanted the stories I had told myself about how I was like my father to continue to be true, not to end and put me into some kind of existential collapse.

But I didn't particularly like my father. He had an explosive temper, he seemed to enjoy ridiculing and shaming me, and aside from his athletic feats he wasn't a particularly competent or resourceful man. He wasn't the kind of father who knew how to fix things, drive a car, give me helpful or useful advice. I wanted to distance myself from his emotional hooks and his incompetent fathering. Not that Abie was any better. If Abie was my father, I would be gaining a kind of freedom, liberating myself from a connection that had never really worked. It would seem that I had merely been a visitor in my family rather than an inmate. I would have a way of understanding my own alienation and my father's weird combination of love and hostility. But then I would have to deal with how it would feel to be the son of someone I liked even less than my father.

The reality of this dilemma was that I was caught between two stories, both of which involved significant people in my life lying to me. Either my parents had lied to me and I wasn't my father's son or Abie had lied to me and I was. Neither scenario was appealing.

I made up my mind to drive to Westport, Connecticut, to see my brother. Having decided not to become the doctor that my parents wanted him to be, he is now a semiretired financial analyst who lives in a comfortable home filled with antiques and collectibles that his wife finds at local garage sales. He fills his spare time with writing projects and has self-published a few detective novels starring a dapper and manly alter ego. Currently, he is translating *Don Quixote*, part of his fascination with great thinkers and writers such as Spinoza, Dr. Johnson, and Thomas Jefferson. He takes his literary interests very seriously, and I think the pleasure they give him made the demands of his professional life easier to handle.

Over bagels and lox that I'd brought from the city, we talked. Gerald recalled how my parents never treated Abie with respect. He said they always seemed angry or disgruntled with Abie. "I don't think they ever had a good word to say about him." But when I asked him why, he couldn't remember anything specific. He felt it was just normal family friction, nothing unique—and certainly nothing to suggest that Abie might have been my father.

When I asked Gerald if he was ever warned not to be like Abie, Gerald simply said, "No, I have no memory of that. They never said anything like that to me."

I couldn't believe this, since that warning had been the endless refrain of my childhood. So I asked again, "Never?"

"No, never."

"Did they ever call you Abie accidentally, just as a slip?"

"Perhaps once or twice."

I, on the other hand, remembered that my father called me Abie all the time. He'd stutter and stumble before coming up with my actual name.

Gerald also recalled that before I was born our parents talked a great deal about having another child. It was a constant topic. If what I had heard from Abie was true, he said, then "they must have

Our family

had an overwhelming desire to have another child," must have been desperate enough to consider artificial insemination as a last resort.

But if they did go the artificial insemination route, why didn't they ever tell me?

"I think they would have been deeply ashamed, would have taken extraordinary precautions to keep you from knowing."

The conversation was a little frustrating because my brother couldn't remember more details and because he seemed so emotionally detached. But that, of course, is in keeping with his more restrained personality. He did say, though, that I had always seemed different from "the family." Apparently it wasn't just my own subjective feeling of difference. I got the sense from him that there was a reality underlying my feeling of not belonging.

On the ride back to the city, I thought about just how different we are. My map of the past is filled with emotional way stations. Every detail, like Proust's madeleine, evokes for me a corresponding affect. My brother, on the other hand, coped with his own upbringing by shutting down. For him feelings are at best optional, at worst destructive. Understandably, because for ten years before I was born he had had to face the difficulty of living with our deaf parents without anyone to share it with. Shutting down might have been a good idea for a boy alone. I, on the other hand, had had him to share my childhood with. He may not have been everything he could have been to me, but he was my brother—someone to whom I could talk and confide my feelings, even if he didn't give me much comfort. With emotions, though, it's often any port in a storm—and he was at least a port even if he couldn't be my haven.

SIX

Going to See the Oracle

WAYNE GRODY KEPT ME INFORMED about the progress of his work on the paraffin-encased fragment of my father. After trying several times to extract DNA without success, he ran out of the sample I had provided and we had to get Columbia to send a few more slices of the original, now dwindling, paraffin block.

The process Wayne was using is called polymerase chain reaction (PCR). It involves removing a minute amount of DNA from the sample I provided. But that amount would not be enough to establish that Morris is or is not my father. In order to have enough DNA to work with, the crucial sequences that will be used in the analysis are then chemically amplified. But the DNA from Morris's paraffin block had apparently deteriorated so much that even when Wayne succeeded in getting it to reproduce via the chemical amplification processes, he wasn't getting a coherent sample. Just when I was beginning to feel that this one chance at using Morris's DNA was going to fail, however, Wayne called me to announce that he had managed to get enough good-quality DNA to give them a "signal." That meant that viable DNA sections were now available for matching with my DNA, and it was time for me to fly out to LA to visit Wayne's lab.

On the way out, I start to read up on artificial insemination and learn some of the history I have presented earlier in this book. That's when it begins to dawn on me that I am not alone, that there are legions of people conceived through this process, many of them no doubt bedeviled by the same issues of secrecy and uncertainty that have been troubling me. It seems like there is a virtual city of lost children out there, and, just as I had recently done, new citizens enter every day, many of us still grappling with whether this is really how we came into being. Most grew up thinking that they were part of a biologically cohesive family and only found out the truth of their origins by accident. Now they are haunted by these absent donors who are their fathers, and they want to find out more. Most won't, but for those who want to go to the trouble and expense, there are Web sites and organizations to help donor offspring, as they are called, locate the men who masturbated them into existence.

I'm feeling a welter of emotions. First there is the excitement and fear of heading toward the answer to my questions. Science will be the final arbiter of this question that's been haunting me. And in a strange way I'll know more than any of the protagonists of this story—my father, mother, Abie. I'll know for sure what they may have only guessed at.

As the plane passes over the Grand Canyon, I marvel at being hurled through space and time to meet my fate, drawn ineluctably toward an elusive oracle that will now at last be forced to speak.

The little hidden bits of me concealed in my cells will finally get their chance to take the witness stand and tell their hidden truth. I'm imagining a sleek, modern laboratory with whirring machines that will provoke the testimony from those cells—and from Morris's. There will be a last judgment and a final hearing when my identity and fate will be sealed.

Flying first class, bumped up by my frequent-flyer points, I'm being well fed and well plied with liquor. But as the constant and obsessive thinker I am, I'm not entirely convinced of the possibility of certainty. If I get a result that shows that Morris is my father, then I still won't know if I was conceived via sexual intercourse with my mother or through artificial insemination. But if it turns out that Morris isn't my father, will I be able to tell who is? It might have been that Abie's semen was only used once in many tries. There might have been other donors.

I try to imagine the scenario as it might have happened. It is a cold winter day, and Morris has gone to Abie's workplace in Manhattan. Morris shows up with a strange request, but Abie, a bit shocked at first, agrees. He takes the small glass vial that Morris hands him and reluctantly heads to the dingy shop bathroom. There he masturbates (with what thoughts in his head?) and ejaculates among the graffiti and the grime, dribbling the tablespoon of semen that contains me into the vial. Love has pitched its mansion in the place of excrement, as Yeats once wrote. Abie walks out sheepishly and hands Morris the bottle, making, perhaps, an offhand comment, a joke, or some lewd observation. My journey in life has begun.

Morris places the vial in his inner pocket to keep it warm against the winter air. He walks briskly, racing style, to the subway and takes it up to Ninety-sixth Street. It's probably a fifteen-minute ride. There he gets out and walks to West End Avenue and Ninety-fourth Street to the offices of Max Sichell, gynecologist. My mother is waiting, perhaps lying on an examining table. Dr. Sichell takes the vial, extracts a few drops of the semen, and injects them into my mother's waiting uterus.

If the scenario goes as explained in the medical books I've been reading, she will return the following day for another insemination. I remember Abie saying "nine months later you were born," which made it sound as though there was only one insemination. But it's more likely there was a second insemination, and sometimes another donor would be used for the second one. Again, according to what I've been reading about artificial insemination, that donor might have been Dr. Sichell himself. Often, in the days before an anonymous donor system was established, the male gynecologist might excuse himself, go into the next room, and return, perhaps slightly red-faced, with the sample. A negative finding, that Morris isn't my father, might lead to the conclusion that the donor was either Abie or someone—anyone—else.

It's a big country out there, and so many people don't know who their fathers are. From up in the stratosphere, you get to take a god's-eye view of things, and looking down at the Grand Canyon as I fly toward Los Angeles, I begin to muse that perhaps it doesn't really matter if one of those microscopic creatures down below has some DNA that is slightly different from what it was assumed to be.

The whole idea of worrying about who your father is seems all of a sudden rather foolish. Can the invisible submicroscopic bits of DNA in the invisible millions of humans down there be of any real consequence?

When I get to Los Angeles, I check into the W Hotel in Westwood near UCLA. The lobby is dimly lit and throbbing with sexy music and light-show projections on the wall. The guests are a combination of professors visiting the university and hip-hop stars with lots of bling. After unpacking, I head for Wayne Grody's office. It's on the palm-tree-studded UCLA campus, which looks more like a country club than an institution of higher learning. There is a California feel to the place that seems to combine the Beach Boys with Einstein. I enter the part of the campus where everyone is wearing white overcoats and speaking the language of "endoscopy" and "atrial fibrillation." Wayne's office is tucked away down a long series of hallways. It's much smaller than I was expecting, the typical academic office, windowless, in this case plastered with movie posters and Academy Award announcements for the films that Wayne has worked on as a science advisor. I guess I was envisioning a larger office, one as grand as my expectations. So now I'm pinning my hopes on the laboratory. Perhaps it will be the magisterial place I've pictured, the fount from which my truth will flow.

As I settle into the chair he offers, Wayne tells me that his usual work is paternity testing, which involves comparing the blood of the alleged father and the child. He points out that in his line of work, all fathers are "alleged" until the testing is complete. In my case, though, he says, this is more like a forensic test, in which a sample from a crime scene is matched to an alleged perpetrator. So what we are doing is halfway between paternity testing and crime analysis?

When Wayne refers to Morris as the "alleged" father I suddenly feel protective and wish Wayne wouldn't use that word. With its crime scene or fraud case overtones, the term *alleged* makes me uncomfortable, and suddenly I don't want Morris to be described that way, even if he turns out not to be my biological father.

Wayne explains that they will be looking for matches or mismatches in the DNA of the two samples. They will be considering areas in the DNA that have a lot of repeats of nucleotides, the basic amino acids that make up the genetic strand. These "stutters" in the DNA are called short tandem repeats (STRs), which have no function and which occur most frequently on that part of the genome known as "junk DNA." But they are not junk at all when it comes to determining paternity. If there are two areas of mismatch between these repetitions, he can safely say that the alleged father is actually not the father at all. Wayne tells me, "You get half your genes from your father and half from your mother, so any mismatch has to come from somewhere." Since in my case I have no doubts about who my mother was, Wayne goes on to say, "If you have a mismatch, then you can assume there was another father beside the alleged one."

"Alleged" can become "definitely not" with a quick glance at a lab readout. I'm a little amazed to think that with three billion pairs of genes in each cell, a mismatch of only two would tell me that Morris isn't my father. The problem comes, says Wayne, when you find matches between all the samples. Then you have to keep looking to see if mismatches exist in other locations on the genome to make sure that the matches aren't just coincidental.

When I ask Wayne if he's gotten philosophical about what he does and what paternity means, given all the time he spends looking at these tiny bits of genetic material, he says: "Yes, I have. It depends how you define paternity. We're looking here at genetic or biological paternity. But to me there's a much more important kind of paternity—societal paternity, or social or familial, the person you are living with and love, and that can be much more important than what we find in the DNA. Many of the cases we do are done for the peace of mind of one or more of the family members." Wayne laughs and adds, "Sometimes for the mother-in-law or whoever is suspicious. But even when we get a mismatch, it doesn't change the social situation. If a child finds out that his father isn't his father, the child still loves the parent. They don't want to break up the family as a result."

I'm wondering if his abstract discussion of the social family will apply to me. Will I still love my father? Will my relation to him be different?

Wayne mentions that since his location is in the Brentwood neighborhood of Los Angeles, many of his cases involve celebrities. He looks knowingly at me, as if he wants to tell me some juicy tidbit of celeb gossip, but he doesn't. Obviously, he can't talk about these in detail.

"The really high-profile cases, we have them come into the clinic after hours. We have cases where there are three or four or five alleged fathers. You go in thinking you know what the real story is and you're always surprised."

Elaborating on the implications of his work, Wayne becomes a bit more contemplative: "In some ways DNA is the most important thing in the universe and in some ways the least important. We are vessels for passing along the DNA, so it doesn't matter what the DNA is as long as you can pass it along. Everything that has led up to that has been selected for in Darwinian evolution. If you believe in 'selfish DNA,' then it doesn't really matter what's in it, just that it got to reproduce itself." Wayne is referring to Richard Dawkins's controversial 1976 book, *The Selfish Gene*, which argues that humans are just vehicles for genes, which Dawkins calls "immortal replicators," to propagate themselves. A gene that benefits its human container will be able to pass along its unique structure to another generation and succeed in spreading it through the gene pool. In other words, you may think you did the deciding in picking your mate, but in fact you are just the hapless tool of your genes selecting a suitable other set of genes. Humans as we evolved didn't necessarily have to exist in the world, but successful replicators do have to exist. We just happen to be most familiar with the containers of today's replicators, which we call plants, animals, and humans.

This discussion makes me think of our genes as little scraps of paper we carry around in an envelope until we mindlessly pass along the contents to the next generation. Or maybe it's more accurate to think of us as the inventions of those little scraps of paper, envelopes they created for the purpose of delivering our gene packets to the next generation of delivery personnel, who will then do their part in keeping the process going, the DNA replicating. Wayne wonders aloud about whom we are passing these genetic messages to. Will there ever be anyone who will be able to read them, finally, and understand what they are saying? Perhaps we in the twenty-first century will be the first people to read the contents of the envelope and be in a position to write back—that is, to change the genome. All of this speculation sets my head spinning. I have to remind myself why I've come here in the first place.

Wayne takes me back to my quest when he cautiously brings up the ethical issue. By probing into Morris's genetic past, am I violating his privacy? Given the new HIPAA laws that protect patients' rights, including the right to privacy, am I simply blundering my way into a very secret and private place where I should never have gone and where I don't belong?

"That's a very important issue," Wayne muses. "It's really in a state of flux. Who should have access to all the stored materials in pathology laboratories around the world? You think of it as just a tiny bit of your father, and it is, but at the DNA level it's your father's entire genome, so someone could access all the information about him on a medical level. When someone has a biopsy, they still own that tissue, and they have the first right to that. In your case, your father's been dead for a long time, so we can't get his informed consent."

Wayne pauses to think a bit more. "I did wrestle with this issue when you first approached me. I think it would have been more difficult if you wanted to have some medical genetic testing that you might want to know for your own health but which would have violated Morris's right to privacy. In the case of paternity, that's one notch lower on my level of concern. It's not a medical issue. But if you were trying to find a medical condition that Morris might have wanted to keep secret, there might be an ethical issue. But even then you might have a right to know as the possible child. In some legal spheres, dead people are not considered human subjects. When it comes to genetic testing and research that has been thrown into doubt. But since you are the next of kin, we are okay. However, some ethicists might have some problems with what you've done."

A kind of Catch-22 occurs to me: if I'm not my father's biological son and haven't been adopted legally, then I am not the next of kin. So perhaps I don't have a legal right. Do I have any claim to the secret buried in his DNA, or am I a kind of high-tech grave robber?

Wayne ponders this point and says, "Who knows how upset Morris might be for you to discover this now, if he had some kind of consciousness? I don't see a huge potential for harm. He's not going to be embarrassed now."

"The dead have no secrets," I find myself saying. And it occurs to me that my parents, in keeping this secret, would have just been following the standard advice of the day. If I was a product of artificial insemination, they would almost certainly have been told by the doctors to keep the secret for my sake. From everything I've read, I know that that's how it was done in the past. By not telling me about my origin, they were simply doing what they saw as their duty by me. But now that I have a say about my own life, shouldn't that give me permission to breach their vow of secrecy?

Wayne seems to agree, pointing out that things have changed and now the child of artificial insemination or adoption has a right to know the identity of his or her parents, especially for health reasons, so that information about any inheritable diseases can be part of the child's medical records. We're rationalizing something that is in a gray zone.

"So you're cool with this?" I ask him.

"Pretty cool. I wouldn't say a hundred percent. About ninety-eight percent."

"What's in the two percent?"

"If I felt it really violated the Hippocratic oath, I definitely wouldn't be involved. Let's just say I've at least thought about this a couple of times—about what your father would think about us doing this. I think I've come to terms with the explanation that this is a legitimate use of this technology, and you are the appropriate person to be requesting it."

We are both trying to steady the moral ground as it wobbles a bit under us. I ask him if he thinks it was wrong for Abie to have told me.

"He felt a need to do this before he died. He obviously felt better for having done it. He waited for your father to have died so as not to embarrass him. Abie must have felt some burden on his shoulders. I think he took a risk. For his peace of mind he upset you. But he may have benefited you from a medical perspective." It's true that now I don't know how to fill out those forms in the doctor's office—the ones that ask you for your family medical history.

I'm thinking about Abie and his courage (can I call it that?) in telling me his version of the story. A few words whispered in my ear, and now I'm in a car riding from Wayne's office to his genetics laboratory, where we are going to attempt to pry open the secrets deep inside a cell of my dead father's body. We arrive at a nondescript building that houses the genetics lab. As we walk into the large, brightly lit room, a hum of equipment greets our ears. This is more like it! The place looks like a classic sci-fi lab. Now I feel that I'm really going to find out—all this technology can't be wrong. I'm sure that visitors to the Delphic oracle must have felt the same thing when they saw the huge marble columns of the Temple of Apollo. Of course, my temple has big computers, blinking monitors, things that look like microwave ovens, and large refrigerators instead of a special chamber devoted to the sibyl. Lab technicians in white coats with gloves on their hands sit at various displays. Earlier Wayne mentioned that film crews routinely come to his lab when they need to shoot footage for genetics-related subjects.

Wayne is talking with his assistant. He's discussing a similar case involving a paraffin block. This one belongs to a living person who had a biopsy and wanted to confirm that the sample used was really from his own body, so Wayne is matching up the DNA in the biopsy with the DNA in the person's blood. Apparently it looks like a match.

I notice that Wayne is scrutinizing a sheet of paper that looks like a seismometer reading or the readout of an EKG, with recurring peaks and valleys. The peaks measure the number of short tandem repeats that have been read by a laser. "What we'll be doing here is comparing the pattern of peaks from your blood and from the paraffin block. If you're Morris's son, the patterns will match up." So when this Delphic sibyl speaks, it won't be in a mystical swoon but in a printout from a computer.

We go into another room. There's a technician using a pipette, a very thin tube of glass, to suck up and measure out minute amounts of DNA. A Chinese American woman with a name too difficult for Wayne to pronounce, she's been renamed J.J. by Wayne, who's taken the acronymic easy route. As she sets up the test to look for the key markers for the paternity test, J.J. shows me my own DNA.

Now I'm face-to-face with the essence of myself. I'm disappointed that it's just a tiny little bit of fluid, about five teardrops' worth at the bottom of a minuscule vial. I was expecting something more impressive in this essence of me. If the old adage "Know thyself" still means anything in this genetic age, then I am defined by this clear, colorless fluid. I have met my self, and my self is nothing more than a vial of tears.

Dawn, another technician in the room with us, had previously removed this DNA from the blood sample I had drawn in Harlem. An attractive woman in her forties, Dawn is now sitting in front of a sterile glass isolation chamber, her hands inside it manipulating a test tube, extracting DNA from another person's blood sample. Dawn explains that she is using a system called Puregene to remove the DNA. This involves introducing various chemicals into the blood sample to dissolve the proteins while preserving the DNA, which is precipitated out. The first step is to lyse cells—that is, to break their cell walls and thus free the cell's contents—because the DNA is trapped within the cell's nucleus. Various other chemicals stabilize the DNA and digest the RNA. Then the unwanted proteins are removed along with other contaminants by salt precipitation. Finally the DNA is precipitated out by using alcohol, and a stabilizer is added to preserve the DNA.

When she's done, the clear liquid has been transformed into what looks like a piece of lint or a tiny white piece of mucus floating in some more clear liquid. It looks underwhelming—tiny and insignificant. I imagine that if I dropped the lint to the floor, I'd never find it. I think: *So your whole being, the triumph of the human genome, is summed up in a little piece of lint.* I guess if you want to be astounded by DNA, you have to think about it on the microscopic level, because it's certainly not impressive on the purely visual level. From that to me—how is it possible? DNA forges our identity, but it is paradoxically both the sum of all the things that make each of us unique and the sum of everything that makes us like all other humans.

Now we go have a look at my father. The lab has received shavings from the original paraffin block. There are ten shavings in a tiny vial. Each shaving is five thousandths of a millimeter thick, and each looks like a very thin fingernail clipping. If I look closely, inside the shaving there is a faint black line. That's him. He's gone now, but here, preserved from 1979, is a tiny piece of him.

As Dawn places the vial back in a drawer with other blocks, I feel a weird sense of loss. There is a strange power to the presence of an individual, whatever form it takes. The simple, mute existence of a part of a loved one's body, no matter how minuscule, resonates in a way I would never have expected. The fact that they are putting even the tiniest part of my father away makes me sad. I'm beginning to understand why some cultures keep the bones of their ancestors at the ready. This must be the attraction of reliquaries containing little bits of saints' bones or teeth or hair, the fragments standing in for the person.

I'm thinking of this bizarre kind of immortality: my father's body is gone, but the bit in the paraffin survives with the DNA intact forever. Or if not forever, for a very long time. DNA remains stable over hundreds, even thousands, of years. We can read DNA from mummies and from dinosaurs.

But when we add up all the information we get from the mummy, what do we know about the person? I remember that at Hobart and William Smith Colleges, where I taught for a couple of years, there was an Egyptian mummy of a young woman in the library. I have no idea why they kept a mummy in the library, but I used to stare at her whenever I went to get a book. She was very beautiful; you could see that even after the process of mummification and the thousands of years that had passed. I almost felt as if I knew her and even felt myself developing a kind of crush on her. The more I looked at her, the longer I stared at her small and delicate face, the more I sensed a kinship with her. But why do we think we can read meaning into the physical details of bodies? Does the face of your lover or child tell you something beyond the chemistry and structure of the proteins and minerals that make it up? And would the mummy's DNA tell me any more than her face could?

Would DNA be able to say if people long gone were humorous or dour, conservative or liberal, gourmets or fast-food addicts? Does the fact that I have twelve repeats of a single nucleotide at one part of my DNA mean anything about who I am or who my father was? Now that we know about DNA, do we need to reconceive of ourselves as huge masses of chemicals, and products of the genes that make those chemicals? We tend to believe that faces *can* be read, but if that's the case, why can't we read our DNA through our faces? Perhaps at a subconscious level we do—and when we select our friends and lovers we are actually just picking the mix of DNA that appeals to our own DNA.

Back in the lab, we move to the next step in this detective process. We are going to take the tiny bit of DNA from me and the other bit from my father and grow them so that we get larger amounts that can be subjected to analysis. This process of growing the DNA is the polymerase chain reaction (PCR) I mentioned earlier, and it involves isolating the fragment of DNA that we want to compare and then making it replicate itself many times. The section of DNA we want to look at is amplified so that it can be mapped.

J.J. is standing in front of a complicated machine that has a tic-tac-toe pattern filled with tiny tubes and looks like a peg game called Hi-Q that we used to play as kids. At the bottom of each tube are the reagent, buffer, and enzymes for the PCR reaction. J.J. takes the pipette and places a small drop in each tube, saying, "Now I'm adding your father's DNA into these." She pushes a small cap on top of each. Then she does the same for mine. Now my DNA is mixing with the reagent. So is my dad's, which looks identical to mine.

J.J. moves quickly, her manner perfunctory. She's blasé about what she's doing. "We have to perform these tasks very fast." No romance here. I'm the son and the writer trying to find meaning and myself in every drop of colorless liquid. But as Wayne the clinician says: "We don't get too emotionally attached." That's fine for him and for J.J., but I have to feel attached to my little part of the human genome. It's going to tell me who I am.

J.J. pushes a few buttons and the machine begins to hum. The black tic-tac-toe-shaped box has the name "DNA Engine" embossed on it, but it is actually called a thermal cycler. It brings the DNA fragments to specific temperatures—94 degrees Fahrenheit, then 60, then 72, and then back again to 94—for specific, sharply limited periods of time. The whole process takes a few hours and the DNA replicates itself a millionfold by the end. What happens as the thermal cycler changes temperatures is a repeated process in which at each temperature stage the DNA strand is endlessly forced to separate, find matching nucleotides, and recombine into two new DNA strands, activated at each stage by chemicals that work only at specific temperatures. It's a kind of sorcerer's apprentice scenario in which more and more brooms are being produced as Mickey Mouse watches in disbelief. This time I'm in Mickey's place staring at a strange sci-fi process in which my dad's dormant DNA is being spurred to life and forced to reproduce. It's not exactly the life of a normal DNA strand in a human body, but it is a form of life, awakened by science from the stillness of death to quicken again. I think of the title of Ibsen's play *When We Dead Awaken*. In the thermal cycler, the tiny fragments of my dad and me are zipping into action, combining and recombining, in a bizarre form of side-by-side reunion. It all feels a bit like Dr. Frankenstein's laboratory reanimating the dead, but it makes me happy that a little bit of life can be restored to something long gone.

After the machine amplifies enough DNA to work with, the lab technicians will put the DNA on a sheet of gel between two glass plates. The gel sheet is then placed in an electrophoresis machine, which is essentially a large box with a white screen. The DNA is located at the bottom of the gel sheet, and electricity is run through the gel, in order to get the nucleotides that make up the short tandem repeats to move up the gel so that a laser can measure the results. Since the DNA has been labeled with fluorescent tags, the laser can reveal how big or small each DNA fragment is by reading the pattern of peaks and valleys created by the movement of the DNA. By comparing my DNA's peaks and valleys with my dad's we can see if they match.

Wayne opens a black loose-leaf binder with various paternity cases. He pulls out one that he has taken the precaution of rendering anonymous. I can see the printout showing the peaks and valleys. Wayne says, "We look at the profiles of the peaks. The instrument measures the size, which tells us which repeat number we have. You can look up the charts and tables and find the frequency of certain short tandem repeat numbers in the ethnic or racial group involved in the family, or you can just eyeball these. When you see the peaks lining up, those would be matches." We are looking at the DNA of four individuals—mother, father, and two children. Wayne says, "Every peak signal in the child had to be inherited from the mother or the father, so we first assign them to the mother since we have no doubt she is the parent." I can easily see peaks on the graph corresponding to heights of three and eight, representing the different STRs.

"The number-three came from the mother," Wayne continues. "The number-eight couldn't come from her, and so it had to come from the father." After I'm able to locate the match quite easily,

Wayne says in a self-deprecating way, "This part isn't rocket science. Anyone can see." Then he adds, "Half your DNA peaks should match with Morris if he really is your father. The other half would match your mother, but we don't have her DNA."

As unambiguous as the readings would appear to be, there are many opportunities for mistakes to be made. Wayne says that they try to be very careful to avoid errors or problems, and the nature of the testing is such that they can usually spot when and where something has gone wrong. For example, the PCR amplification may fail, especially if it didn't get properly started. This is more likely to happen with old DNA from paraffin blocks, because the DNA is often fragmented or degraded. Morris's paraffin block is twenty-five years old, and Wayne says that his block "is getting up there as far as this kind of study goes." Although DNA is relatively stable, not every region you want is accessible. When parts are missing, the problem is called "allele dropout." In that case one of the signals might be lost, or the results could be "dirty." Or it might be that one set of nucleotides started to "stutter" when they were reproducing.

Of course the worst nightmare is sample mix-ups. Every lab takes great pains to ensure that samples are clearly labeled and properly stored. Wayne reassures me, "Yours is one we've been keeping a special eye on. So that wouldn't happen." But he also reiterates his concern that Morris's DNA may not be of high enough quality because of how old it is.

"What's the next step?" I ask.

Wayne tells me that the normal turnaround time is about three weeks. But in this case, the advanced age of Morris's DNA means that some of the STR markers they normally use may not be readable, due to allele dropout. So they may have to repeat the procedures, and it's hard for him to predict how long it will take to get what they need.

"When do you think I will know something?" I ask with a note of desperation in my voice.

"We could get in touch with you in four to six weeks." Wayne retreats to his professional voice. "But it might not work out at all. We'll just have to see. We'll send a FedEx letter to your home."

I'm feeling a bit shaky and nervous now. I've come so far, only to realize that maybe I won't find out anything after all this. I'll have come all the way to the oracle and gotten the brush-off.

Wayne and I shake hands and say goodbye. After I leave the lab I sit outside under the palm trees of the UCLA campus, listening to the birds and thinking about what I have seen. The first thing that occurs to me is how impersonal the lab is. If I was expecting the lab to have the aura of the kind of place from which an oracle might speak, I was wrong. The machines and equipment make it seem purely functional. I guess science can't be as impressive as a sibyl. And then there was the letdown of seeing my own DNA. Somehow I had expected to feel a jolt of recognition or insight at seeing myself writ small in DNA. But the sample had nothing special about it. It didn't seem particular to me. How could I have any feelings about a small smudge of genomic material that resembled a piece of lint?

Perhaps the lesson is that the body, while it seems to be unique to those of us living in one, isn't really. It's universal. Everything I'm looking at right now—the palm trees, the birds, the white-coated doctors walking around—is made up of DNA. And with minor variations, all human bodies are essentially alike, because there is a human genome that is common to all of us. Even the percentage of DNA we share with chimps is astonishingly large. It is now estimated that nearly 99 percent of the DNA in humans and chimps is identical.

The little piece of material I stared at in the test tube is something so similar to everyone else's DNA that I'm wondering if it really matters whether it's my uncle's short tandem repeats or Morris's that are in me. Whoever they came from, they are just little building blocks and not much more than that. What's important is who I am and how the DNA is expressed in me, how I walk and talk, how I move through the world and interact with those I love. This is far more important than the identity of a microscopic arrangement of nucleotides. At least that is how it feels to me at the moment.

So the oracle, like all oracles, turns out to be Delphic. You're always going to have to interpret the meaning of the prediction. My plight is no different from that of King Croesus, who asked the Delphic oracle if he would win a particular battle. The oracle replied that if he entered the fray, "a great empire would fall." Croesus was thrilled with the prediction and charged ahead. But in the end he lost the battle and his kingdom, confirming the oracle's prediction that a great empire would fall. He just hadn't understood that the empire to fall would be his own. The trick is in knowing how to interpret the prophecy or the data. Will I?

Now I'm thinking that while I'm not attached to the outcome of what the DNA reveals—whether it's Morris or Abie who turns out to be my father—I do care about knowing the simple facts of my story. What is important to me is to find out whether my parents were locked into this terrible secret that they felt they had to keep. I need to know so that I can discern what the secret meant, for them and ultimately for me. When the letter from Wayne arrives, with what I hope will be the information I've been seeking, I'll do the interpreting.

SEVEN

Tracking Down the DNA

IT TURNS OUT THAT I AM NOT ALONE in wanting to use DNA to find out about my life. More and more people are trying to find out their heritage by taking DNA samples, usually from cheek swabs, and sending them off to places that promise to determine if one has Zulu or Cherokee heritage, or whether one's people come from the Fertile Crescent or the Hebrides. Our DNA, it seems, is the secret trace of lives lived elsewhere, the bodily signature of relatives long gone, a ghostly track following migrations from a distant past. It may also prophesy the ailments that will plague us or our children in the future. Even beyond wanting to know whether I was Morris's or Abie's son, I was now eager to have this other information, too, to understand more about my family, its life, its history, its medical legacy.

In recent years yet another use has been found for DNA: to exonerate prisoners who have languished in jail for years, accused of crimes, particularly rape and murder, that they did not commit. And then there are those celebrity paternity cases that have garnered so much press. In Mick Jagger's case, DNA testing led to the rock star agreeing to pay $35,000 a month to twenty-nine-year-old Brazilian underwear model Luciana Morad, who had given birth to Jagger's seventh child, Lucas. In the paternity case brought after Anna Nicole Smith's death, custody of her child was given to former boyfriend Larry Birkhead when DNA testing proved him to be the biological father.

Paternity testing may be relevant to people in other ways as well. A woman who had grown up with suspicions that her godfather might have been her father recently contacted me to tell me her story. When she reached fifty, she developed a rare genetic disorder. She was puzzled because no one in her family had this problem, and her doctor assured her that there had to be someone who had passed it on to her. Having read about DNA testing, this woman—let's call her Laura—decided she'd try it. One day when Laura was visiting her godfather, she went into his bathroom and removed his traveling toothbrush, some hairs from his comb, and beard clippings she'd emptied from his electric razor. She sent the materials to a DNA lab, and the results that came back a month later showed that her godfather was in fact her biological father. When she confronted him with the evidence, he admitted he was her parent. She said that when she stared across the table into his eyes at that moment she realized for the first time that she was staring into her own blue eyes, and all the previously inexplicable moments in her life suddenly slipped into alignment.

Most of us understand that we can use DNA analysis to find out about our genetic legacies, our parentage, and our ethnicity. But the majority of people believe in DNA without really understanding what it is, just as we believe in lightning without really understanding how it happens. It's a lot easier to take a cheek swab than it is to conceive of the biochemical processes that lead to a test result and interpretation. When I started to go down the road of DNA testing, I, like everyone else I knew, was fairly ignorant of the technology involved in paternity and family heritage testing. I had to educate myself on the basics.

Telling you what I learned will help you follow my detective story about myself, but much more important, it will enable you to understand how you, I, and all the rest of us fit together in the great human story of evolution and migration. My story about my desire to find out who I am and who my parents were is just one instance of the curiosity almost everyone feels about who and where we come from. Thanks to DNA, we can now begin to unravel much of the mystery of our origins—of our family, our people, and our species.

With all big stories, we have to begin with the smallest details—in this case the genes, which have locked in their contents the clues to what we are seeking. Long before the discovery of the gene, people were aware of the existence of inherited traits. It doesn't take any knowledge of science to realize that children often look like their parents and that plants grown from seeds look like the plants that produced those seeds. But there were varying theories to explain those similarities. Some felt that environment shaped appearance, others that the mother's womb and even her state of mind created her offspring's qualities. It was widely believed in the Middle Ages and the Renaissance that if a mother saw strawberries while she was pregnant, for example, her child would have red hair or a red birthmark. If she was frightened, she might have a child with a disability.

One of the first major scientific advances toward understanding genetic inheritance was made by Gregor Mendel, a serious, bespectacled nineteenth-century monk who looked like an accountant. He was the first to work out the math behind the mystery of inheritance and to come up with the idea of dominant and recessive traits. Living at a Silesian monastery in what is now the Czech Republic, Mendel took up gardening, a passion from his childhood. In the monastery's garden he grew sweet peas, and he noticed a pattern in the appearance of different-colored flowers as he crossbred these plants. Mendel guessed that there was some substance that was passed from parent plant to offspring, and by experimenting with more than twenty-eight thousand multicolored sweet peas, he found he could predict which offspring would be which color. He came up with two laws of inheritance. The first one postulates that some inherited traits are dominant while others are recessive, causing three out of four offspring to have the dominant trait while the fourth would have the recessive one. Mendel's other law dictates that each inherited trait is independent of other traits. For example, blue eyes do not always come with blond hair. Although his work was influential in developing the concept of the gene, Mendel himself never used the term, being content to suggest that some unspecified factor had to be transmitted between parent and child.

The easiest way to understand the terms associated with DNA and the kind of testing I want to do on my father's tissues and my own is to think about the biggest units first and then work down to the smaller ones. Obviously, the biggest unit in genetics that concerns us here is the human being. Humans have obvious traits—such as the color of our hair, eyes, and skin; our build and height; our facial features; and so on. We also have traits that are less directly obvious, such as intelligence, body chemistry, immune system functioning, blood type, and so on. All of these are determined, in some major way, by our DNA.

The next step down from the entire human are the structural parts of the body (the muscle and bones) as well as the interconnecting nervous system and the organs (lungs, stomach, liver, kidneys, brain, skin, etc.). These discrete parts are in turn made up of smaller units visible only through a microscope and known as cells, each one of which is composed of even smaller structures. The specific structure that concerns us is the nucleus of the cell, a small area in the center of the cell that is walled off by a membrane. Within each cell's nucleus is the genome, which is the full package of our genetic matter. When cells reproduce, which they do by the process of splitting or mitosis, they replicate the genetic contents of each nucleus. So the genetic material in each cell is passed along intact to the succeeding generations of cells. Through this process, the full complement of genes is reproduced in every cell—except in those that make up the sperm and the egg. In sperm and eggs, a different kind of cell reproduction occurs, which results in only half of each parent's genetic material being passed along. This means that each child will receive half its genetic material from one parent and half from the other.

Craig Venter, the handsome, brash, and entrepreneurial geneticist whose company helped decode the human genome, has been in the news because of his laboratory's success in providing the best and most detailed analysis of a single human genome—and not just any genome but specifically Venter's own. Few other human beings have had their genome analyzed in such detail. Venter's genome, like that of all of us, is made up of twenty-three pairs of chromosomes, the next smaller units within the cell nucleus. These chromosomes are actually long strands of DNA that are normally invisible, even when observed with a microscope, but at the moment the cells divide, the DNA clumps together into separate and visible units that can be stained to make them visible. It's because of their ability to absorb stain that they are known as chromosomes (literally "colored bodies").

On each chromosome are the even smaller units called genes. These are the parts of the DNA that manufacture one of twenty specific amino acids. When these amino acids are linked together in chains they form proteins. Let's say, for example, that one location on the chromosome is involved in the making of beta globin, which is one of the proteins necessary to the production of hemoglobin, the substance that transports oxygen in the blood and makes it red. A gene may control just one process—the manufacture of the amino acids used to make the protein beta globin. If you turn the gene on, it sets in motion the complicated process by which the DNA makes RNA, which makes beta globin, which ultimately makes hemoglobin; if you turn the gene off, it won't.

An allele is any of the alternative forms of a gene that may occur at a specific spot on the chromosome. Eye color, for example, is determined by alleles. You need two alleles—one from each of your parents—to determine the color of your eyes. Your light-brown-eyed dad and your dark-brown-eyed mom will each give you an allele, and your eye color will be the result of these two different alleles, which will combine in the way that Gregor Mendel described for recessive and dominant traits. Genes are like the cartridges in a printer. Some genes have only one form; these are like a black cartridge that produces only one color of print. Alleles, however, are like the different color cartridges that can mix and create different colors depending on the combinations.

Getting down to even smaller levels than the genes and alleles are nucleotides, which are the building blocks of the nucleic acids—DNA (deoxyribonucleic acid) and RNA (ribonucleic acid). Piecing together an understanding of nucleotides took a long time.

The word *gene* came into use at the beginning of the twentieth century as a shortening of the term *pangene*. Charles Darwin had developed the idea of pangenesis to help explain how heredity fits into evolution. The theory of pangenesis held that each cell in the body shed *gemmules*, little particles of inheritable material. These collected in the reproductive cells, and so each cell in the body had a "vote" or role to play in determining the offspring. In effect, each cell competed with every other cell in a Darwinian way to create the traits of new offspring. Wilhelm Johannsen, a Danish botanist, coined the word *gene* in the first decade of the twentieth century as a shortening of pangene (he also invented the terms *genotype* and *phenotype*). Others had been using the terms *factor, unit factor,* or even *id* to describe this mysterious and elusive "thing" that transmitted hereditary traits. In 1910 Thomas Hunt Morgan, an American embryologist, established that genes were located on the chromosomes.

Although researchers now knew there were genes, they mistakenly assumed that genes must be proteins of some kind. It wasn't until three scientists from the Rockefeller Institute wrote a paper in 1944 that the protein theory was laid to rest. The three medical

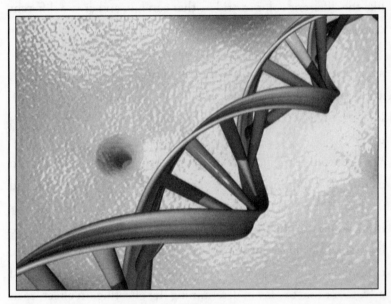

The double helix

researchers, Oswald Avery, Colin MacLeod, and Maclyn McCarty, determined that it was nucleic acid and not protein that carried what they called the "transforming factor." Although DNA and RNA had been discovered and described before, no one had specified that these substances were the transforming factor in genetic inheritance. Avery, MacLeod, and McCarty identified them as such but had no idea how they actually worked.

Seven years went by and no one succeeded in figuring out how the nucleic acids passed along the genetic code. That wouldn't happen until after Rosalind Franklin was able to take X-ray diffraction photos of DNA, which occurred in 1951. Two years later Francis Crick and James Watson, the two wunderkinds of genetics, using Franklin's X-rays, figured out the workings of DNA, which were revealed to an astonished world through the famous drawing of the double helix. Initially created by Crick's wife, Odile, who was an artist, no drawing ever entered human consciousness with such force as did that of the double helix.

What Watson and Crick worked out was that DNA was a double helix made up of two long parallel twisting chains of sugars that form the sides of the structure, with a series of pairs of nucleotides linking the sides. To visualize this, imagine a spiral stairway. The sides of the stairway are the sugars, and the steps are the nucleotides. The two pairs of nucleotides that make up each step are called base pairs, and there are only four different kinds of nucleotides: adenine, guanine, thymine, and cytosine.

These four possible components of the base pairs don't attach to each other in random fashion. Adenine will only attach to thymine, and guanine will only link up with cytosine. Thus, each of the steps of the circular stairway can only be made up of adenine-thymine or guanine-cytosine pairs. In keeping with the stairway analogy, one might think about the steps as being made of four different kinds of wood; that would mean that the steps would always be glued together at their middle in some specific combination—say, pine-mahogany or oak-walnut. You could switch things around from left to right for variety and make the steps mahogany-pine or walnut-oak, but you could never make a step out of pine-oak or walnut-mahogany. If you were designing your steps to make them look interesting and varied, you would have only four possibilities— pine-mahogany, mahogany-pine, walnut-oak, or oak-walnut.

The amazing thing about DNA is that, as complex as life is, the construction of life on the genetic level is very simple, just the combination of these four nucleotides arranged in very limited ways: adenine-thymine, thymine-adenine, cytosine-guanine, or guanine-cytosine. (They're easier to see as abbreviations: AT, TA, CG, GC.)

A gene, then, is made up of a specific number of steps on the very, very long stairway—let's say, just for example, from the fifth step to the tenth step. We call that part of the staircase a gene because we've discovered that a particular protein is made from the code embodied in the repeated nucleotides on these and only these steps of the staircase. In the case of beta globin, for example, the gene to make that protein is 576 base pairs long. If we wrote it, here's what it would look like:

ATGGTGCACCTGACTCCTGAGGAGAAGTCTGCG
GTTACTGCCCTGTGGGGCAAGGTGAACGTGGAT
GAAGTTGGTGGTGAGGCCCTGGGCAGGCTGCT
GGTGGTCTACCCTTGGACCCAGAGGTTC
TTTGAGTCCTTTGGGGATCTGTCCACTCCTGATG
CAGTTATGGGCAACCCTAAGGTGAAGGCTCATG
GCAAGAAAGTGCTCGGTGCCTTTAGTGATGGC

CTGGCTCACCTGGACAACCTCAAGGGCAC
CTTTGCCACACTGAGTGAGCTGCACTGTGA
CAAGCTGCACGTGGATCCTGAGAACT
TCAGGCTCCTGGGCAACGTGCTGGTCTGTGT
GCTGGCCCATCACTTTGGCAAAGAATTC
ACCCCACCAGTGCAGGCTGCCTATCAGAAAGTG
GTGGCTGGTGTGGCTAATGCCCTGGCCCACAAG
TATCACTAAGCTCGCTTTCTTGCTGTCCAATTTC
TATTAAAGGTTCCTTTGTTCCCTAAGTCCAACTAC
TAAACTGGGGGATATTATGAAGGGCCTTGAG
CATCTGGATTCTGCCTAATAAAAAACATT
TATTTTCATTGC

How does the mere repetition of four different nucleotides in so few combinations—AT, TA, CG, GC—ever result in the creation of all the complicated proteins that make up our bodies? Where the complexity of life comes in is in the manner in which the four nucleotides are repeated. To take a very simple example of the diversity that can arise from very limited forms of expression, when I say "Yeah" it means I agree with you, but when I say "Yeah, yeah" it can mean that I doubt what you are saying. "Yeah, yeah, yeah," as in the Beatles song "She Loves You," eliminates the doubt and just emphasizes that she *really* loves you. And "Yeah, yeah, yeah, yeah" means "I don't *think* so!" In effect, repetition changes the meaning of the single word. Likewise, the repetition of the nucleotides begins to create chemical meaning or structure. Morse code is another example of how two simple units, dots and dashes, can be used to generate an infinite array of meanings. And a more contemporary analogy is with digital systems, another kind of code. The digital technology that produces HDTV and streams Beethoven's Fifth to your iPod is basically one that uses repetitions of the digits 0 and 1 in complex arrangements.

DNA, then, is a very long strand of information made up of the repetition of the base pairs. The entirety of this long strand will make up one chromosome. Just to give you a sense of how long a strand of DNA can be, the largest single human chromosome is made up of 220 million base pairs. The shortest is about 50 million. And these are only two of twenty-three pairs of chromosomes. Astoundingly, the total of three billion base pairs in the human genome occurs in every single cell in the body (with the exception of sperm and eggs, as explained earlier). That is three billion base pairs in the nucleus of each cell multiplied by the number of cells in your body, which is approximately fifty trillion. I'll let you do the math!

To recap (and this is a little like the old song about the knee bone being connected to the thigh bone): Cells have chromosomes inside their nuclei. Chromosomes are strands of DNA. Genes are locations on the strands of DNA. Alleles are alternative forms of a gene. And nucleotides are the building blocks that make up these very long strands. The nucleotides interact with forms of RNA to produce amino acids. A complex series of events involving RNA strings the amino acids together to form proteins, which in turn form the larger structures in the body—muscles, bones, organs, and so on. In short, the DNA acts as a blueprint or set of instructions for the making of human beings.

The very idea that there is some kind of individuality or identity in this massive swarm of chemicals is a kind of wonder. Perhaps even more remarkable is that each mass of cells and genetic matter we call a human being seems to want to find out how it came to be, what its life is about, and who the people were who passed on to it the chemicals that make it what it is. The compulsion to locate the source of our uniqueness seems all but universal. And yet 99.5 percent of all human DNA is the same. (We used to say that 99.9 percent was the same, but now that Craig Venter's DNA has been analyzed in excruciating detail we can see that he has forty thousand variations from another person's DNA.)

So it's in this 0.5 percent of our DNA that is different that we find the key to identity. In other words, our identity isn't found in the part of the DNA that is the same as everyone else's, but in the tiny percentage that differs. And that tiny percentage tends to be located in the nonfunctioning part of the genome. Of the three billion base pairs that make up the human genome, there are only about twenty thousand to twenty-five thousand genes that function to create proteins. In any given chromosome, then, most of the nucleotide repetitions don't seem to do anything or make anything, and it's within those repetitions—the ones that are not vital to our functioning—that we find the source of most of our variations and differences.

The reason that most of the variations are found in the nonfunctioning or "junk" area of the chromosome is fairly obvious. It's really important that all the functional DNA get passed along from generation to generation unchanged. If it does change, the chances that the resulting mutation will turn out to be good for the organism are very slim. Mutations are rarely beneficial. In short, it's in our vital functions that we all need to be a lot like each other, not distinctive. On the other hand, it doesn't matter that much to evolution and survival if the nonfunctional parts of the genome change, since they don't really do anything. Thus there is evolutionary pressure on the functional genes not to mutate (except under certain circumstances), but there isn't much pressure on the nonfunctional part of the genome to remain unchanged. To use an analogy to make things clearer: it's critical that your house have a roof, walls, a foundation, and certain other basic features that provide shelter and protection. As houses have evolved over time, those features have remained constant. But the color of your inside walls isn't particularly important to keeping the elements or your enemies out; neither are the lighting fixtures, the materials of the floor, or the type of couch you have. Consider the nonfunctional parts of the DNA to be like the chintz on the armchairs.

The changes in the nonfunctional parts of the DNA can happen if there is a kind of stutter when DNA reproduces itself. A bit of the DNA strand can get doubled back on itself and the resulting transcription can repeat a sequence. Sometimes the sequence can repeat quite a few times. It is these relatively short sequences of repetitions—called short tandem repeats, or STRs, which I mentioned earlier—that have been used in genetic testing to establish identity. They tend to occur at particular locations in the genome, and the combination of these repeats acts as the unique fingerprint that can identify an individual.

In addition to STRs, there is another way of "fingerprinting" us genetically: single-nucleotide polymorphisms (SNPs). Rather than a series of repeats, these are differences that operate because one nucleotide is substituted for another. SNPs are about substitutions in the genetic code, while STRs are about repetitions in the code. If we made the analogy with speech, STRs would be stutters, in which the word or letter was repeated, while SNPs would be slips of the tongue, in which one word or letter was substituted for another.

The most common alteration, which occurs in every one hundred to three hundred base pairs out of the three billion base pairs that make up the human genome, is for C to replace T. For an alteration to be considered an SNP it has to occur in at least 1 percent of the human population; within the entire human genome, there are about ten million SNPs. If we looked at a single chromosome, we might find a group of related SNPs that we could group together as a unit, and that identifiable grouping of SNPs would be called a haplotype.

With both STRs and SNPs, the uniqueness of the pattern—of repetitions (in the case of STRs) or substitutions (in the case of SNPs)—is the fingerprint that distinguishes my DNA from yours. The ability to find these distinguishing features, the DNA fingerprint, is what makes identification of an individual almost 100 percent accurate. But the use of DNA testing goes beyond simply identifying individuals, telling you whether or not they are part of your family. It can also be used to provide information about your family's origins.

For example, a group of African Americans who had been told the family legend that Thomas Jefferson was their ancestor decided to investigate their heritage. They had pressed their claim to be considered the descendants of Jefferson and his mixed-race slave Sally Hemings, but the Jefferson family had resisted. Genealogical research had gone just so far, so the group turned to DNA testing. The results were unmistakable, proving incontrovertibly that the African Americans were related to the Jefferson family through the male line. The genealogical evidence combined with the DNA results strongly suggest that Jefferson himself was the common ancestor of these descendants.

DNA analysis has also been put to use by researchers who have been trying to determine the family origins of Christopher Columbus. He has been variously reported as being of Italian, Portuguese, or Spanish descent, and also rumored to have been Jewish. In 2004, Spanish geneticist Dr. José A. Lorente obtained genetic material from a cache of bones in a cemetery plot in Seville where Columbus is believed by many to be buried. Since then researchers, including Francesc Albardaner, a Barcelona architect, have tried to match the DNA in these bones with individuals whose family name is Colom or Colombo. Albardaner has taken hundreds of cheek swabs from males with these family names. The idea is that if the DNA from the Coloms and Colombos matches that of the bones, it will be a good guess that these bones really are Columbus's. So far no official results have been released. But if the DNA is determined to be that of Columbus, then Y chromosome tests could be done and we should also be able to find out if Columbus was of Jewish patrilineal descent.

In this and other cases, haplotyping is used to determine family and geographical origin. On a recent PBS program, the African American scholar Henry Louis Gates Jr. used the National Human Genome Center, a DNA lab run by geneticist Rick Kittles, who was then at Howard University, to find out if Oprah Winfrey, among others, was descended from Zulu warriors, as she had been told. Kittles is a handsome man in his forties with a shaved head and wire-framed glasses. He started his laboratory out of a desire to find his own origins. Kittles discovered that his female line goes back to northern Nigeria, the land of the Hausa people. He noted, "I then went to Nigeria and talked to people and learned a lot about the Hausa's culture and tradition. That gave me a sense about who I am. In a way, it grounded me. Two people there looked like cousins I have—they even behaved like them!" Kittles eventually decided to launch a for-profit side business helping people learn more about their ancestry. His was the first to specialize in serving the African diaspora.

Testing Winfrey's DNA, Kittles found that her family stories were correct and that her haplotype matched those from Zulus living today. But Gates himself, who is the director of the W. E. B. Du Bois Institute for African and African American Research at Harvard, discovered that his female line wasn't African at all but of European and possibly Jewish origin.

How do Rick Kittles and other geneticists discover this long-buried family history? To explain how this process works, we need to understand something about how genes are transmitted from generation to generation via our reproductive cells. Genetic information is passed along by the eggs in a woman's ovaries and the sperm in a man's testes. Humans have twenty-three pairs of chromosomes that contain an individual's DNA, and those same twenty-three pairs are in every cell of the individual's body—except the sperm and egg. Here's why: If a sperm and egg each consisted of twenty-three pairs of chromosomes and they united to form a child, the child would end up having double the proper number of chromosomes—forty-six pairs of chromosomes instead of twenty-three. In the next generation that number would double again, and so on, ad infinitum. To avoid this endless multiplication, eggs and sperm undergo a unique kind of cell division. Instead of the usual process by which cells divide, which results in the exact number of chromosomes being replicated, reproductive cells split up their pairs of chromosomes, so that each sperm or egg cell has only twenty-three chromosomes—not twenty-three *pairs* of chromosomes. It's as if each egg went through its closet and threw out the match to twenty-three pairs of socks. But luckily, the sperm also threw out the matches to its twenty-three pairs of socks, and when it joined up with the egg, the two combined their socks and ended up with twenty-three full pairs again.

Continuing the sock analogy, let's say that each time ordinary cells divide there is a slight mixing up of genetic matter, so that the new socks are always different in very minor ways—different-colored threads here and there, small deviations in the patterns, and the like. In genetics this is called recombination, and it describes the way that pairs of chromosomes can shuffle and exchange bits of genetic material between them. After many generations of these variations, however, the sets of socks might come to look considerably different from their forerunners. This is actually the case with DNA, particularly in the nonfunctional units. The result of all the re-sorting, repeating, and substitution over time is that if you compare your DNA with that of your relative from twenty generations back, it might be hard to establish an exact match.

However, there are two parts of the DNA that don't change much if at all. It turns out, conveniently for those of us who want to find out about our family's origins, that these almost unchanging bits of DNA are found in discrete places in the father's and the mother's genetic information: in the DNA from the Y chromosome of the father and the DNA from the mitochondria of the mother.

The Y chromosome is part of the twenty-third chromosome pair of the male, and it differs from the corresponding chromosome of the female. In females, the two chromosomes that make up the twenty-third pair both look like X's and are exact matches, but in males one of the X's is missing a leg, so it looks like a Y (hence the name). Genetically, we can tell if someone is biologically male or female by looking at this twenty-third pair, although there are some exceptions. A person may have an XY chromosome arrangement rather than the XX arrangement that is standard for females. This would mean that the person is genetically a male but has what is called androgen insensitivity. In cases like this, the person has a vagina but not fully formed female reproductive organs.

The interesting thing about the Y chromosome is that, unlike all the other chromosomes, it is extremely resistant to change through recombination. For obvious evolutionary reasons, the Y chromosome never recombines with the X part of the pair. Since the Y chromosome determines maleness, it would be problematic for evolution if the Y or male chromosome just periodically combined with the X or female one—at least from the point of view of reproduction. Nature doesn't want to mess around in any significant way with the state of maleness, otherwise humans might have no males to fertilize females. The stability of the Y chromosome means that the chromosome is handed down from father to son without any significant changes, and is therefore a unique fingerprint that gives us an excellent way to determine paternity as well as long-term family origins.

On the female side, the part of the DNA that doesn't change is located in the mitochondria. Mitochondria are little organelles inside each cell that act as the battery or powerhouse providing energy for the function of the cell. It is believed that they were originally, at the dawn of life, freestanding bacteria that invaded or were engulfed by some cell. But rather than destroying or being destroyed by each other, the bacteria and the cell worked out a symbiotic relationship, with the bacteria (now mitochondria) providing energy, and the cell providing a consistent environment and protection. Because mitochondria are their own organisms, rather than belonging to the cell, they also carry their own unique DNA. And because the mitochondria's DNA is hermetically sealed off from the cell's DNA, their DNA does not recombine with the cell's genetic material. What this means is that, like the Y chromosome, the mitochondrial DNA is passed along relatively unchanged from parent to child.

But the mitochondrial DNA is always from the mother, not the father. Although sperm have mitochondria and therefore mitochondrial DNA, the moment the sperm enters the egg, the egg destroys the sperm's mitochondrial DNA. The result is that every human carries in his or her mitochondrial DNA only the record of the maternal family line.

Geneticists talk about a "mitochondrial Eve," who is the most recent common ancestor of all humans on earth today. She lived about 140,000 years ago in the region of what is now Ethiopia, Kenya, and Tanzania. While no one has found her bones, there are mathematical formulas that allow us to trace the commonality between all of the mitochondrial DNA we carry back to a single woman. When we try to follow our ancestry through DNA testing, we're not going so far back, but attempting to identify branches of families that descended from a recent common ancestor.

Although neither the Y chromosome nor the mitochondrial DNA recombines with other genetic material, they do mutate over time, as does all genetic material. The rate of these mutations is steady and predictable, which also allows us to estimate quite accurately how long it has been since two given people last had a common ancestor. This in turn means that geneticists can tell how long it was since a certain mutation took place and can therefore plot the changes in a group of people over time.

Let's say a group of people with the same Y chromosome or mitochondrial DNA left a specific region, such as Africa, thousands of years ago. All of them would have the same pattern of SNPs or STRs; in other words, they would have the same haplotype. Then perhaps one of them underwent a significant change in haplotype. If we look at that person—let's call him Charley—he'd have the same pattern of DNA with the exception of this one change. We could, of course, tell that Charley came from the out-of-Africa group because his DNA would match that of the group. But we'd also be able to tell which subsequent generations came from Charley and which came from the rest of the out-of-Africa group, because Charley's descendants would have the out-of-Africa pattern plus the specific Charley haplotype pattern as well. By carefully noting all the patterns we could come up with a haplotype map that showed us various groupings around the world as well as the history of how those groups came into existence. That's the essence of how we use DNA to assign people to different groupings. Geneticists have been assembling a map of the diaspora of these haplotypes, which they call the "HapMap" for short.

In my quest, I've used DNA testing to find STRs, and the result of that will tell me if Morris is my father or not. I'll also be using Y chromosome testing and haplotyping to reveal what can be known about the male line of my family. In the course of that testing, I'll find out the origins and history of that family over a period of thousands of years.

EIGHT

Opening the Letter and Finding the Truth

I'VE BEEN EDGY. I thought it would take about four to six weeks or so after I visited Wayne's lab in California before I heard anything, but there have been problems in reading the DNA. Wayne let me know that there was a poor signal, and that other problems had arisen in the polymerase chain reaction. Because of these mishaps, Wayne had to start the process all over again, and to do so he needed yet another set of shavings from the original paraffin block.

I called Columbia University Medical Center to request another sample. This time they were much quicker and promptly sent off a new batch from the block, but the second round of waiting for the DNA analysis to be repeated is even harder. So much of this experience has been about waiting. I am now worrying that I won't be able to get the clear and incontrovertible DNA reading I was expecting. I was so hopeful, and now it seems that the oracle might let me down. I am beginning to despair, since how long can that paraffin block hold out? How many little scrapings are possible from such a minute amount of tissue? Won't they eventually run out of Morris's DNA? My sense is that this round will probably be the last. Just when I was beginning to think I might get an answer, the truth seems to be receding into the great obscurity that has hidden it till now. Perhaps it is true that you really can't grab hold of the solid silence of history and expect it to speak, even if you have the strong arm of science at your side.

But then, after repeated, increasingly desperate e-mail queries to Wayne, I do finally receive a response—he now has an answer that he'll send me by FedEx, as we agreed earlier. At last the envelope arrives. My wife calls me and hands it to me, giving me an expectant and sympathetic look. My hands shake when I pick up this bland-looking envelope, knowing that inside I will find the answer to the obsessive question I have been asking.

I take the letter to my study in the attic and sit in an armchair all by myself, staring at the envelope. I realize I'm going to find out who my father is. The answer is just sitting in this envelope. Suddenly I realize that I'm incredibly nervous, as if I am standing on the edge of a cliff, about to plunge into something shocking and deep. I feel as if I'm facing my own execution. In a sense I am, since the former me may be undone.

The what-ifs begin to race through my mind. What if I find out that Morris is in reality my father? That in some way is an answer that I dread. It will mean that I have been agonizing all this time over something that was a figment of my uncle's deranged imagination or, even more disturbing, of his malign intent. I'll have disrupted the lives of my brother and my family, stirred up muddy waters, and, worst of all, believed my parents to have been liars when they weren't.

However, if I find out that Morris isn't my father, I'll feel justified that all my broodings did make sense. But then I'll have to come to terms with Abie's being my real father, which might be even more troubling than all my other concerns.

This, then, is the moment of decision. All the scenarios I've unrolled will come down to a simple judgment, like a death sentence, or a reprieve: *He's your father. He's not your father.*

Both excited and full of dread, I say to myself, "Let's find out."

I open the envelope. And like all good puzzles, the mystery continues in the form of Chinese boxes. Just to ramp up the suspense level, there is another envelope inside the first. I have that Academy Award moment feeling: *The envelope, please!* I imagine that everyone I ever knew is waiting for me to open it up and find out. An audience full of relatives and friends is looking on expectantly as my hands tremble. I slit the inner envelope, and my destiny spills out like lifeblood. The letter is on Wayne's official letterhead and reads:

We are writing to tell you that we have now concluded paternity testing. Results indicate that Morris is excluded as a possible father of yours by mismatches we have observed. We find a DNA pattern in the child that is not present in the DNA of the alleged father so it must have been another man.

So this is it—my father is *not* my father. He is just an "alleged" father.

An initial feeling of deep sadness sweeps over me. I find myself saying the words "excluded as a possible father" out loud. But they are mere words, and I have to repeat them again and again so that they will coalesce into meaning. Now Morris is just the guy who raised me—a surrogate father, the man who is lounging around the house, the extra man. We're not biologically related as father and son anymore, and suddenly I have to perform the difficult mental act of reenvisioning him as my uncle—as Abie was.

What I feel at the moment is abandonment, as if my father—Morris—had suddenly packed up and left me. He went away and is no longer my dad, absconding with his paternity and my connection to him. My father died today all over again. I've lost him. And I don't even have an idealized father from central casting to replace him with. Just the undesirable Abie, who is far from the ideal. In the classic family romance, when the child imagines himself to be someone else's son, he conjures up a king or a great artist or a rock star—not some shady character like Abie.

My feelings are shifting like winds, from second to second, minute to minute, and now the feeling of abandonment suddenly morphs into one of triumph. I say, "I knew it! I just knew it! All the things I felt throughout my childhood—that I wasn't part of my family, that I was the one who was always left out, who was considered bad for being 'other'—have turned out to be true." I'm almost exultant.

Then I start thinking about my parents. My mother probably had it easier because she knew I was her child, the creation of her own body, but my father would have had a more difficult time. I find myself feeling sorry for him and all the pain he must have had to go through after my birth. I'm trying to imagine what it must have been like for him to have to keep up the pretense: smiling and

Eva (pregnant with me) and Morris

handing out cigars to the men in the family, including of course Abie, all the while knowing that he wasn't the father; laughing heartily at the inevitable nudge-nudge jokes about how he'd finally "risen" to the occasion after ten years of trying; listening to all the people who found resemblances to him in my baby face. I remember how he'd tell me that I had my grandfather's broad shoulders. He could have been sure of that resemblance, at least, even if Abie was my biological father.

Thinking about the sacrifice he made to have me, I suddenly feel a new sense of appreciation and love for him. Morris did a great job at keeping his secret. He had to hide these seriously wounded feelings because he believed that was the way to protect me. Both my parents went to their graves thinking that they had succeeded in doing right by me, despite the cost to themselves. They never dreamed that I would ever discover the truth.

And now through this amazing technology of DNA testing, I know. They say the truth will set you free, and all of a sudden I am feeling really free. I know something more about myself, and no one can contradict what I've felt all along. I feel like someone born into a new life.

That state lasts about ten minutes, and then my bubble of triumph bursts and I feel myself slipping into a state of total shock. After all, if you have been living with one story about your life for more than half a century and then you suddenly have to reassess that story, now accommodating a major new piece of information, the results can be traumatic. It's as though the life story I knew had been carefully and painstakingly carved on a giant granite wall, and now all of a sudden I'm desperately trying to stick this little pink Post-it on it. And the little note is not really sticking. I keep finding myself saying "Okay, now I've got to get the DNA test results," as I have been for months, and realizing a moment later that I've already got them.

I've been so involved in my own feelings, I have forgotten to tell those who also need to know. I go downstairs and inform my wife of the outcome. She has been waiting to hear from me ever since she saw me take the letter upstairs what now seems like hours ago. She comforts me, but I can see that she is as shocked as I am. I've been pursuing the question of my origins for so long that she had just gotten used to the existence of this ongoing, open-ended project, and my having actually arrived at the answer I'd been seeking is something that takes our breath away. I tell my children, who seem interested but not bowled over, since they never knew Morris or Eva. They were both dead by the time my son was one, before my daughter was even born.

Now it's time to pick up the phone and call my brother. "Gerald, I just found out...he's not my father."

There's a long pause and then my brother says in a mechanical voice, "I'm surprised. I didn't expect that. But as far as I'm concerned it doesn't change anything between us."

"It doesn't change anything for you," I say, "but it changes a lot for me. He's not my father. And you and I are half brothers."

"You're still my full brother as far as I'm concerned."

"Of course I am still your full brother, because I grew up with you."

"I feel like I want to give you a hug."

I'm surprised by Gerald's display of emotion—he's usually quite guarded—and I appreciate it.

"Are you going to test Leslie to be sure?"

"I am sure, and now I don't need to go any farther."

"Well, I still love you."

"I love you, too. You're the only brother I know."

He is trying to say nothing has changed, but it has. Because of the confidences I've shared with him and the support he's given me on my journey to the truth, our connection seems stronger now than before. But the fact remains that he is my half brother, not my full brother.

Having told my wife, my children, and my brother, the conversation I most wish I could have is with my parents. Since they are not around, I run a movie in my head about what would happen if I could summon them back to life and talk to them. I walk into their one-bedroom apartment in the Inwood section of Manhattan. Passing through the front door, I find myself in the living room with its old, familiar royal blue, plastic-covered couch, next to the window that faced the back of another apartment building. Then I hear my parents rattling about in the dining alcove, where the pastel wallpaper depicts scenes from Venice. Sitting down at the table, my elbows resting on its vinyl tablecloth, I gaze at the gondola passing beneath the Rialto Bridge as Eva asks me about the children and offers me some inedible, badly cooked food.

Then I say, in sign language, "I just found out something very important. I found out all about your secret." They look at each other nervously. "I know everything."

"Know what? What do you know?" They try to maintain an appearance of innocence, but the façade is giving way.

"I know about the artificial insemination. I know I'm not Morris's son."

And then the truth is out, released like some high-pressure geyser held for eons under the earth.

I think at that point I'd probably start to cry, and they would, too. And then we'd all hug each other. But I'd want to say to them, "It's okay. You did all right. You did what the doctors told you to do because they thought it would be devastating for me to know. But I'm not devastated. I'm saddened by the way this story had to play out for you and me. But I love you...very much. Even more because you went the extra mile. You fought the idea that you couldn't have children. Most people would have just adopted. You took this amazing step. You were willing to risk your self-esteem and face the condemnation of relatives and friends if they ever found out. You used the latest technology. You had my crazy uncle give his semen. That must have been hard. And you did it so you could have me, the little crying baby who would come back years later and say, 'I found you out.' You did that because you really, really wanted me. So thank you, thank you, thank you for doing the impossible and for having me, because I wouldn't be here now if all those steps you took had never happened."

Of course, I can't ever have this discussion with them, but as I leave the movie theater of my mind, I am thinking how true it is that you can't fool a kid. It's a cliché to say that children have antennae that always pick up on what's going on in the family, even if

The "sensitive" one

they can't articulate the messages they are receiving, but clichés come into being for a reason. A young child is like the family dog that feels all the emotions in the house as it lies on its doggy bed and furrows its brow. My family always called me "too sensitive" when I was a kid. I wonder if they were afraid that my sensitivity was actually a response to something real. Like a weather instrument, I was detecting unseen phenomena in the atmosphere. My mother and father and even my brother were pretending it was fair weather, but I was picking up the storm.

NINE

Family Romance, or Who Is My Father?

I HAD BEEN THINKING ALL ALONG that the choice for me was between Abie and Morris. If Morris wasn't my dad, then Abie would be. But Wayne mentioned in a subsequent conversation with me that the DNA analysis indicated Morris's DNA was so different from mine that it was unlikely that he was even my uncle. If Morris were my uncle, I would share some of his DNA, since brothers have at least 50 percent of their genetic material in common. To be more precise: for Morris to be my uncle, at least three of the markers in my test should have been shared with him, as Wayne explained, but they weren't. Of course, it is possible that even without the three markers, Morris could still be my uncle. Wayne was invoking only the most common scenario.

This led to a whole new set of conjectures just when I was thinking that I'd solved the secret of my origin. Now I knew for sure that Morris wasn't my father—but if he wasn't my uncle, either, that suggested that Abie wasn't my father. And if Abie wasn't, then who was?

The research I had done on the early days of donor insemination in the United States revealed that it was frequently the gynecologist himself who provided the semen. This impromptu technique was often the rule before there were established norms and procedures, at a time when there were no sperm banks and the art of preserving semen had not been perfected. It wasn't known then that semen could be frozen without damage, as it is now, when it is routinely sent by overnight mail in cold packs for easy home use. It was so much more convenient, if somewhat unethical from our current perspective, for the gynecologist to excuse himself from the room, masturbate into a container, and return to inseminate the patient lying on the examining table. This technique was far simpler than trying to arrange for anonymous donors to drop off samples a half hour before the woman showed up. And then of course there was the possibly narcissistic, machismo element involved in fathering scores of children.

Now I am beginning to wonder again about my mother's gynecologist. Thanks to the fact that Morris was compulsive and kept a notebook of all his expenses, and thanks to the signature on my birth certificate, I know that the doctor who delivered me was Max Sichell. He was an upscale West End Avenue physician who had merited a *New York Times* obituary stating that he "departed suddenly" on March 6, 1966, that he had been born in Berlin, and that he was a "noted obstetrician and gynecologist" on two continents. He was survived by his wife, Dr. Jane Sichell, a brother, a brother-in-law, an uncle, and a cousin. There was no mention of any children. He and his wife, who was a psychiatrist, had apparently opted to spend a life devoted to their clients. Or perhaps she was infertile.

How perfect! He had no children, so of course he'd want to have a child. And that child could have been me. This makes so much sense. My ugly-duckling scenario becomes even clearer. No wonder I am so smart, was so interested in science and medicine from an early age, so unlike the rest of my family and my relatives! I am Max Sichell's son. I'd read about the physicians who had started insemination clinics and filled their sperm banks with the deposits of Nobel laureates, doctors, writers, and the generally above-average men who had accomplished much in their lives. Here, now, am I—the product of just such a scenario.

I imagine how, even assuming that Abie's story was correct, this could have happened. Let's say that Abie told the truth and his semen, mixed with Morris's, was used on day one of the insemination process. But I had read that it was common for the patient to return for several days in a row during her time of fertility to be inseminated repeatedly. One gynecologist who performed inseminations in the 1950s and 1960s wrote that since "we prefer at least two inseminations during the ovulation period and call upon several donors to supply the semen, we never are able to establish the source of the effective sperm." This "firing squad" approach was perfect for establishing and maintaining donor anonymity—that is, before DNA testing came on the scene.

So my mom might have been inseminated on the first day with the Davis brothers' mixed seed, but then on day two or day three,

Dr. Sichell might have slipped into the anteroom to produce what would turn out to be the effective impregnating semen—his own. This scenario was even more likely since in those days one of the purposes of artificial insemination was the eugenic goal of improving the human race. Like the eugenic expert I came across in my reading, who emphasized the importance of having the donors be men of science or medicine, Sichell might have figured it was for the betterment of humanity for a doctor of some accomplishment to father the child of a deaf working-class couple.

Here it is, then—I am the offspring not of a poor, uneducated Polish Jew but of a richer, smarter German Jew, one step up in the immigrant hierarchy. And to complete the dream of every Jewish boy, I am the son of a famous doctor, not the son of a lowly factory worker. I am not the grandson of a fishmonger. No, I come from a long line of German Jewish professionals—doctors, lawyers, even perhaps scholars. I have a completely new sense of entitlement. I find myself smiling at doctors and admiring hospitals. I feel elevated above the common masses.

To prove this connection with Sichell, I begin trying to track down any of his relatives. I've noticed that his name was spelled sometimes with one *L* and sometimes with two. I begin combing the obituaries and sending e-mails to anyone with that family name. I want to find some male Sichell relative whose Y chromosome could be tested. Or at least I want to find a photograph of my doctor dad to see if we resemble each other. I contact all the medical schools in Berlin trying to get his school photo. Initially, I come up with nothing.

When I type his name into the Internet, the only thing I find is a Web site that links him to a "Gotham Hospital." A discussion board related to New York City history lists a number of people who are tickled that they were born in "Batman's hospital." The conversation is of the random, desultory kind found throughout the Internet, but there is one entry of interest to me. Someone named Christina Bürgi had written:

> I too was born in Gotham Hospital in June 1950. The address given by evid2 [a previous poster] is correct. My father took a picture of the building in 1950. I had also looked up the address in the Internet before I visited New York in April 2002. I took another picture. The building was still there then. My mother's doctor's name was Dr. Max J. Sichell.

How interesting that he and I should have the same middle initial. Could this be another clue?

Christina posted this note a month before I notice it. Unfortunately, she left no return e-mail address. I have no reason to believe she'll be checking this obscure Web site again. I mean, who really cares about the name of a hospital from fifty years ago? I write to the Webmaster of this list, who says that the site does not keep the addresses of posters. So I post the following message on the list:

> Christina mentions that Dr. Max Sichell was her mother's doctor. He was my mother's doctor too. I was born in Wadsworth Hospital in Manhattan in 1949. I'm trying to find out more about Max Sichell. Do you have any further information?

I check the Web site for a few days, and then I see this post from Christina:

Re: Dr. Max Sichell: Dr. Sichell was originally German, from Berlin, I think. His wife was a psychiatrist. Will try to find out more from my mother. He visited us a couple of times here in Switzerland. I have a picture of him if you are interested.

Interested? Yes, certainly I am. Christina and I correspond. It turns out that Sichell was a family friend. She sends me two photographs of him. And she casually mentions that he was Marlene Dietrich's gynecologist. That clinches it for me. I am one speculum away from the star of *The Blue Angel*. Christina also tells me that Sichell had loved to drive around New York City in his Cadillac, and he'd apparently died in a car accident. This all seems to fit perfectly into my newly evolving life story. Sichell was a famous doctor, my mother and Dietrich were his clients, and both my mother and he had died prematurely in car accidents. We had the same middle initial. Surely someone out there is writing my story.

When I look at the photograph, I feel a kinship. He seems immediately appealing, friendly, welcoming. We don't look particularly alike, but then there are the eyes. I enlarge the picture on my computer and put a picture of me next to it. Yes, the eyes are similar.

Dr. Sichell looks like the dad I wanted. This is no Morris or Abie—this is my real dad. The one who deserved me, and whom I deserved. Plus his wife—let's call her my stepmother—looks like a smart, sassy, and interesting lady. And a psychiatrist, no less!

Dr. Max Sichell and his psychiatrist wife

I begin to remember things about Max Sichell. My mother always mentioned his name with affection and reverence. I suddenly have a memory of accompanying my mother to Dr. Sichell's office when I was very young, perhaps five or six. I recall the Manhattan location and my mother introducing me to him. I recall his friendly hello to me, and I also remember that when he died in 1966 my mother was very upset. Now this all made sense. He is my father. I was brought to see him, perhaps more than once, so he could watch me grow up. And of course my mother would mourn his passing, since he was the man who had impregnated her.

In trying to find out if there are any living relatives of Max Sichell on whom I could run a DNA test, I stumble upon some interesting Web sites. These are sites devoted to donor offspring who are trying to find their fathers and also to find any half siblings who came from the same donors. It occurs to me that if Sichell had provided his semen for me, he could have provided it for others, too. I contact www.donorsiblingregistry.com and sign up to see if anyone on the list has traced his or her paternity back to Dr. Sichell. I note that many people have found their half siblings and their donors, but most of them were conceived relatively recently through well-known sperm banks that keep records. All they'd have to post is the year of their birth and the name of the sperm bank. In my case the situation is more difficult. In the past doctors were told to destroy any paperwork, since utmost secrecy was the rule.

As a result of putting my name on these lists, I am contacted by Janice Stevens Botsford, a pleasant-looking woman in her fifties, who tells me that she and her brother, Barry Stevens, are actively involved in trying to find their donor. Both of them were born in England in the 1950s, close to my birth year of 1949, and their parents, like mine, were British. Their father's first marriage had ended in divorce because of his infertility. When he married their mother on the next go-round, the newlyweds both understood that artificial insemination would be the only way for them to have children. Interestingly, the father was a physician, who happened to be the doctor for the archbishop of Canterbury—the same man who had commissioned a very damning study on the ethical and religious implications of artificial insemination around that time. Nonetheless, Barry and Janice's parents opted to try donor insemination. The clinic they chose was the one in London run by Mary Barton, a physician, and her husband, Bertold Wiesner, a scientist with a degree in physiology. I remember from my research on artificial insemination that this was the clinic that had recruited a circle of geniuses to act as donors. The inseminations had produced hundreds, perhaps thousands of children, including Barry and Janice.

When Barry and Janice were in their teens, the parents moved the family to Canada, perhaps to keep the secret of their conception from coming out. Or perhaps they wanted to prevent the children from accidentally meeting and marrying offspring from the same donor. This insemination was kept a deep family secret until their father died, when Janice was twenty-two and Barry eighteen. At that time, their mother, feeling that she could no longer keep the secret, especially since she knew that it could affect their understanding of their medical histories, which could be important for them in later life, took them aside and told them the truth. They were both donor offspring, she said, both of them from the same donor, who Barton had told them was Jewish.

Janice tells me that their mother had tried to explain everything in the most loving terms. But Janice and Barry had been shocked at the news, and they kept the revelation private for a long time, sharing it with only a few people with whom they were very close.

About twenty years later, when Janice had children of her

own, she became interested in finding out who the donor might be. Internet resources and the advances that had occurred in DNA testing suddenly made the impossible seem possible. Her mother had told her that Barton and Wiesner had destroyed all the clinic records and that she should leave well enough alone. But Janice continued on with her research. Barry was less interested initially but later became involved and eventually made a documentary film about their story for the Canadian Broadcasting Corporation. The movie, titled *Offspring*, depicts Barry and Janice actively trying to sift through the numerous men who made semen donations at the clinic, including Bertold Wiesner himself, who was a European Jew. In the course of the film, Barry notes that many people discouraged him from his search, but explains that he felt he had to pursue the truth, because not knowing your parent is "like missing the first chapter in a book or looking in a mirror and there's part of you not reflected." That's exactly the feeling I've had all along.

Once Barry and Janice became involved in the donor offspring network, they located a man in England named David, whose parents had also used Barton and Wiesner's clinic. DNA tests indicated that Janice and Barry were half siblings to David, and the film follows them as they go to England to meet him. The three hit it off so well they say that they feel like long-separated siblings, and their families, too, become very close. Together they explore the various geniuses and intellectuals who made up the roster of donors for Barton and Wiesner.

Throughout the film, we are struck by how much Barry resembles Wiesner (whose photograph we are shown), even down to their hairlines, while Janice does not. Barry is a tall, thin man with a high forehead and black hair. Janice is shorter and rounder and has very different features. It seems hard to imagine they are full siblings, but their mother had emphasized that they shared the same donor. Barry comes to feel sure that Wiesner must be their father. By the end of the film, however, we learn that although David has a positive DNA match with Wiesner, Barry and Janice do not. Barry's desire for Wiesner to be his father was just as strong as my wish that Sichell be mine. But Barry appears to be wrong, and I realize that I might be as well.

However, the story told in *Offspring* wasn't complete. Barry and Janice eventually found out that their initial DNA tests had been poorly done. They also discovered that they aren't full siblings. In fact, the assumption that they were had thrown off their research. In the end, it turns out that Barry is indeed Wiesner's offspring, which means that Barry and David really are half brothers. Janice's donor was discovered to be the scientist Derek Richter. Barry, Janice, and David remain close despite the shifts in their understandings of who is related to whom and how. Even though David and Janice are not half siblings, she says that she still feels connected to him because her brother, Barry, shares the same donor.

There is a vast network of donor offspring from Barton and Wiesner's clinic, although Janice has only managed to locate about fifteen at this point. She, Barry, and David have become active advocates for overturning secrecy with regard to donors, and David has been instrumental in pushing the Human Tissue and Embryos Bill through Parliament in the United Kingdom with a "need for father" provision built into the language. This trend continues in other countries; for example, as of 2005, New Zealand requires that fertility services must maintain records of donors and provide access upon request.

The story that Barry and Janice tell sounds very much like my own. Their parents, like mine and so many others, were advised never to tell their child the truth of their origins because the results could be "devastating." An expert in 1948 wrote that such explanations to a child "might inflict severe psychological injury and increased insecurity." Barry and Janice feel, however, that it was the secrecy itself that had a negative impact on their lives, and experts today tend to follow that line of thinking. Now, most donor offspring sites call for openness and honesty. By 2007, typical Web sites were offering advice like this:

It is never too early to begin telling your child the circumstances of her conception and birth. Small children love to hear the story of their beginnings and often ask to have it repeated. Don't worry about having the right language or perfect terminology. The way you tell this story should reflect the way you always speak in your house, with the same tone, length, and level of seriousness. When the story of the donor-conception is told from the beginning of your child's life, the information becomes embedded in the relationship between your child and you. It is shared and it is a non-event, compared to the experience of disclosing the information for the first time at a later date.

The current approach, which was spurred on by the advent of DNA testing as well as the activism of donor offspring such as

Janice, Barry, and David, is very open and frank. The approach my parents were sworn to—don't tell anyone because the shame and embarrassment of being found to be a "test tube baby" will be so great—is a relic of the past, its effects described quite accurately (at least in my own case) on a twenty-first-century Web site:

> Some children who had not yet been told that they were donor-conceived reported that they already felt different within their families, based on either physical characteristics or personality. They lacked facts to substantiate their strong feelings. Even without being told, children often pick up hidden clues from the family. In the studies that have been completed with donor-conceived children, many reported a powerful sense that some valuable information was being withheld from them.

You could say that my persistence in trying to get to the bottom of my origins is a kind of psychological reaction to a life lived with a secret and a lie, and a long history of sensing that something was amiss.

As I try to pin fatherhood on Max Sichell, I still have that dreaded element of doubt. I can't prove for sure that Sichell is my father. But there is a way to prove that he *might* be. I can do that by using Y chromosome DNA testing to see if I am part of the male line of the Davis family. Since the Y chromosome is passed from father to son relatively unchanged, if I match the Davis family Y chromosome pattern, then Abie would have to be my father, since Morris has been ruled out. But if I don't match it, then Sichell could have been my father. I now decide to do Y chromosome tests on Leslie and Gerald, as well as on my second cousin Frank Davis, who descends from my paternal grandfather Solomon's brother, Abraham.

Frank is a relative who only recently came to light. Coincidentally, while I was beginning to track down my origins, I had received an e-mail from someone claiming to be related to me. Her name was Carol Stirk, and she lived in Australia. Her brother Frank Davis lived in New Zealand. She told me that she was an amateur genealogist and that her researches indicated that our grandfathers were brothers. At first I was skeptical since I had never known of this branch of the family. In my paranoia I worried that this was going to turn out to be some kind of Nigerian Internet swindle. But Carol explained that she had always been told that there was a deaf race-walker in the family, and had used that fact to help her do her research. She found my family by Googling "deaf American Jewish race-walker Davis" and got a Web site with a picture and history of Morris. She followed the information on the site and found me. She had family photos and family stories to prove the connection. I subsequently became friendly with her brother, my second cousin Frank, and his wife, who often came to the United States on work-related travel and looked me up on one of their trips.

When I ask Gerald, Leslie, and Frank if I can do a Y chromosome test on them, they all agree, happy to help me on my quest. Gerald is a little concerned about breach of privacy and opts to keep his results secret from everyone but me, but the two others are happy to allow their results to be part of various databases maintained by Family Tree DNA and other genealogical groups.

The funny thing about doubt is that you never get over it. You can work very hard to eliminate all possible doubt, but if you have a really good obsession like mine, mere facts will never make it disappear. At the same time that I am researching my paternity, I am also actually writing a scholarly book on the subject of obsession, and particularly OCD. So I'm well aware that one of the personality traits of people with OCD is that even though they may be sure of something, they still doubt it. The classic illustration of this would be with the kind of person they call a "checker." Checkers have to make sure that doors are locked, windows secured, gas jets turned off, and the like. They may wake up at night feeling the need to check. Once having been assured that the gas jet is off, they will return to bed. But then they will lie in bed and wonder if they really checked properly, so they'll have to get up and check again. Most people only check once or twice at the most, but checkers can spend hours a day confirming and reconfirming what they believe they saw or did.

Am I a glorified checker? As I keep trying to find the truth, each step of the way I feel confident that it is within my grasp. But then the doubts come back. Now, assured by Wayne's STR test that Morris was not my father, I should just accept the results and assume that Abie's story was true and that he was my biological father, but I have further doubts. Perhaps Abie had not been the donor whose sperm finally made it to the egg from which I grew. A Y chromosome test would give me information that Wayne's STR test could not. Although Wayne's test could rule out a specific parent, as it had ruled out Morris, it couldn't tell me anything about who my father might be or about my specific relation to the Davis family. Of course, if I could have gotten a specimen of Abie's DNA, Wayne's test could have been used to confirm that Abie was my father. Barring that possibility, the Y chromosome test would provide more information. As a compulsive checker, I have to check out this option.

To do this test, I have located a company called Family Tree DNA, run by Bennett Greenspan, which was the same organization that had ultimately performed the correct and revealing Y chromosome test for Barry, Janice, and David. I arrange to have a telephone interview with Greenspan. On the phone, he's a fast-talking Yankee peddler type with a self-deprecating sense of humor. From his publicity photos, I can see that he is a bald man in his mid-fifties with mad-scientist hair flying around his temples. When I first contact him, I assume he is a scientist, but he immediately lets me know that he is a businessman, not a scientist. Before starting Family Tree DNA in 2000 he had owned and run a photo supply outfit, but seeing the digital writing on the wall, he sold the business for a nice profit and started his genetics company. He's a man who is definitely ahead of the curve.

Initially, Bennett had been interested in his own family genealogy. Having located some possible relatives in Buenos Aires, he wanted concrete proof that there was a connection. He did a Y chromosome test and found a match. Some more Y chromosome tests found more relatives and widened his circle of inquiry. Greenspan became convinced at this point that DNA testing was a business and a service whose time had come. In setting up such a business, he would help amateur genealogists and others trying to find their family's origins.

As Greenspan explains to me in our phone conversation, the administrative functions of his company are conducted in Houston, where he lives, but he has the lab work done at the University of Arizona. Although he has now hired some geneticists to work with him in the modern, generic building where he has his own office, this is a place of business, with none of the whirring, buzzing atmosphere of the lab that Wayne Grody runs.

With Bennett's help, I can find out if there is a possibility that Dr. Sichell was my father. If I descended from the Sichells or any other non-Davis family line, then I'll have a very different Y chromosome from my brother and cousins.

Family Tree DNA sends a kit that requires a cheek swab. To get the sample, you rub a small brush against the inside of your cheek for one minute. A surprising amount of cottonish-looking material accumulates on the brush, and then that material is placed in a vial with liquid. You need to take a few samples to make sure that one sample isn't contaminated or incomplete. As with all DNA tests, the search for STRs is done on certain regions in the nonfunctional DNA. These specific areas or segments of the DNA are known as "markers." A person can choose to examine anywhere from twelve to seventy-two markers with Family Tree DNA. The more markers you compare with someone else, the more information you will get about the degree to which you may be related.

I first have a twelve-marker test done on myself and Gerald, who I now consider my half brother. I choose to test only twelve markers because I assume that if we match on all twelve, we will not need to look further—that would indicate that we are in the same family line and would be a definite sign that I am a Davis.

I have to wait for the results, which take more than a month. When the results come in, Gerald and I match up on eleven of the twelve markers. This result is definitive enough to establish that I share the Davis family Y chromosome, which, of course, immediately rules out Max Sichell as my father. My dream of a noble lineage crashes on the shoals of science. This is a difficult fantasy to let go of, but the DNA speaks the truth.

The fact that Gerald and I don't match on all twelve markers confirms—again—that Morris was not my father. If we shared the same father, we would match exactly. Perhaps the marker test on Leslie, by revealing an exact match, will give me the smoking gun I need to prove with great certainty that Abie was my father. To continue the investigation, then, I have a twelve-marker test done on Leslie and also on my second cousin Frank. Again, a month passes, and then an e-mail message informs me that the results are in. All three of us are identical on all twelve markers. This reconfirms that I am a Davis and that Dr. Sichell could not have been my father, but it raises a question: why do I match up exactly with my cousin Leslie and my second cousin Frank, but on only eleven of the twelve markers with Gerald?

I decide, in my obsessive way, to go further down the testing path. Family Tree DNA offers a thirty-six-marker test, which I run on my DNA and Gerald's. That test shows us matching up on thirty-five of thirty-six markers, with the same mismatched marker as before. This means that a slight mutation in the Davis line developed, either in Morris's generation or in Gerald's. According to the e-mail I receive from Bennett Greenspan:

I've looked at the 4 samples and Gerald has a single mutation
from the 3 others . . . meaning that the sperm that fathered him
got the change, while the ancestral marker value is an 11 rather
than the 12 that he has.

Bennett's reference to the "ancestral marker value" being
eleven means that Les, Frank, and I have eleven repeats in this particular location, called 392, but Gerald has one more repeat. This
rather subtle point could well be another proof—if I needed it—
that Abie was my father and Morris could not have been. However,
it would only be a proof if it could be established that the mutation
first occurred in Morris, not in Gerald. Although Greenspan as-
sumes that the "sperm that fathered him got the change," this is, after all, only an assumption. If Morris developed the mutation, then
it would have been passed on to Gerald (but obviously not to me,
since I was not his son) and presumably to Gerald's son, Peter, too.

A side benefit of this Y chromosome test is that I learn about
the geographical origins of the Davis family. Like those folks using
DNA testing to find out if they have African heritage, I can track,
through these results, the Davis family's migration patterns. It
turns out that we have the haplotype known as J2, which shows
that I'm of Jewish and Middle Eastern origin. We of course had
known we were of Jewish extraction, but the fact that we came
from a specific place in the Middle East is a surprise. What I find
out about the J2 haplotype group is that it began in the northern
part of the Fertile Crescent, today's Jordan, Syria, and Iraq, and
then spread through central Asia, the Mediterranean, and India.

Family Tree DNA has a service that lists the findings of everyone's chromosome test on a few genealogical Web sites (unless a person decides to opt out for privacy reasons, as did Gerald). Within days I begin hearing from people whose DNA matches mine to some degree. A genetic genealogist who gave only the name of Ted contacts me with maps and charts to show that my particular subhaplotype originated in Damascus, Syria, then migrated to Toledo, Spain, in the 1200s. When the Inquisition began and the Jews were persecuted and then expelled from Spain in 1492, many Jews went to Germany, Eastern Europe, or Mexico.

A woman named Judy Simon gets in touch with me because the Y chromosome DNA I had tested for my family also matched her family's. Family Tree DNA has its own "surname project." People with the same surname share their information about their genetic background and also their genealogical information. By mapping genetic and genealogical research onto each other, you can draw conclusions to extend the information provided by DNA testing alone. If, for example, you can link up two contemporary families by their genetic signature, you can assume they share the same ancestors in the past, including any ancestors that were discovered through archival rather than genetic research. Judy is interested in contacting me, even though our surnames are different, because her family shares significant haplotypes with mine, and both families appear to have been Sephardic Jews before they moved to Eastern Europe and became assimilated with the Ashkenazi Jews there.

A word on my family name. We had always thought that the name was a shortening of Davidowitz or Davidson. But I learn otherwise from Carol Stirk, the Davis family genealogist in Australia, who tells me that the original family name had actually been Melamedavitz or the Russianized version Melandovitch. So it appears that the name Davis had been shortened by cutting off the first part of the original name, not the last.

My Y chromosome testing connections produce additional information, too. Judy Simon puts me in touch with a Yiddish genealogical scholar named Schelly Talalay Dardashti. Schelly is a New Yorker who was the Jewish genealogy columnist for the *Jerusalem Post*'s City Lights/Metro weekly and writes on genealogy. Confirming what both Ted and Judy told me about the geographic origins of my family, and shedding light on what Carol told me about our family name, she points out that the name, which is Sephardic, not Ashkenazic, is based on the word *melamed*, which means "teacher." The Polish diminutive that had been added later, *-ovitz* or *-avitz*, means "son of." Therefore, Melamedavitz means "son of a teacher." Schelly writes, "According to Pere Bonnin's book *Sangre Judia*, there is a record of a MELAMED in 1487 Toledo." Although the word *melamed* can be used generically, the fact that it is used as a family name in this reference gives a stronger basis to the idea that my family was in Toledo in this period. This observation corresponds nicely with Ted's genetic information about a Bartolome Sanchez, who was born in what is now New Mexico around 1500, and who shares my haplotype. The offspring of Jews expelled from Spain in 1492, which was when almost all the Spanish Jews left Spain, Sanchez could have been part of a large group of crypto-Jews who secretly practiced their religion in the New World. Ted came up with another genetic match for a Jew named Haim Lisbona, who was born in Damascus, Syria, in 1710. His name also indicates a Sephardic origin, since it was common for Jews to take the name of the city in which they lived, again connecting my DNA line to the Iberian Peninsula.

With all this information, I have learned much more about my family than I had known, including the fact that the male line of the family was of the tribe of Levi. Carol Stirk tells me that her grandfather Abraham, my grandfather Sol's brother, was a Levi. She writes that her grandfather was listed as "Avraham ben Moshe HaLevi" on his marriage certificate. The Levites were of the priestly class, but not as elevated as the Cohans, who were the actual priests. The duties of the Levites in the Temple included singing during services, acting as teachers and judges, and also translating and explaining the Torah when it was publicly read. The fact that the family name meant "teacher" would fit into this historical role. There is currently a DNA test to determine if one is a Cohan, which finds the so-called Cohanim haplotype. But there isn't yet one for the Levites. Here I'm relying on my cousin's own genealogical work.

Even though I am disappointed not to be Dr. Sichell's offspring, I am beginning to appreciate my own family's rich and impressive history. And of course my being a teacher now seems to be in keeping with what I have learned about the Davis family being Levites. My passion for knowledge may simply be a fulfillment of the role my family played in the Temple.

DNA gives us all the ability to develop a detailed family narrative. In the past only the aristocracy and the rich had family archivists and inherited documents to prove their long ancestry. But DNA testing means that one doesn't necessarily have to descend from people of wealth or nobility to discover one's origins. It teaches us that everyone has a traceable ancestry, and that no family is any "older" than any other one.

I've learned so much, but I am not finished yet. All indications seem to point to the fact that I am Abie's son. But I still don't have absolute proof. What I do know is that I am not Morris's son. Or is that the case? What if the paraffin block was not really Morris's? What if the hospital had switched blocks back in 1979? Or what if the current staff had given me the wrong block or the block of a different Morris Davis? All of these may be overly obsessive ruminations, but if I want absolute certainty, I'll need to retest the DNA from Morris to analyze his Y chromosome specifically. That will also allow me to see if Morris had the mutation on the 392 locus that Gerald has but that I and the rest of the males in my family line don't have. The problem is, where do I find some other source of DNA? The only source I've come up with thus far is the paraffin block. I'd read that other objects could contain DNA. The most promising of these would be a toothbrush, a razor blade, a pipe, clothing, hair samples, and anything that might contain saliva.

I'd saved some letters that Morris had written to me over the years. But more important, I have the envelopes those letters had come in, which Morris would have licked in order to seal them. Although Wayne had told me that his lab couldn't extract the

DNA from those envelopes, he said that a forensics lab could. So I have gotten in touch with a forensics lab I found online. It is the DNA Diagnostics Center in Fairfield, Ohio, and its director, Dr. Michael Baird, had just done the tests that established the identity of the father of Anna Nicole Smith's baby.

This lab agrees to try to extract the DNA from some of the envelopes I'd saved. At DNA Diagnostics I am working with Dr. Julie Heinig, the assistant lab director in the forensics section. She is an attractive, even-keeled woman with blondish hair and a winning smile, whose sense of humor is of the self-deprecating type. You'd never know that she spends her days working on crime scene materials. Before DNA Diagnostics, she was employed for a few years at the Cayuga, New York, coroner's office, an experience that she compares to working in Dr. Frankenstein's mansion. It was an old, creaky place with a nineteenth-century dissecting theater. She saw more dead bodies and homicides than the average TV watcher.

How did a nice girl like her end up working with dead bodies? I wonder. She tells me that she did dissections in college and never minded the blood and gore. She found herself drawn to the science and got a Ph.D. in applied genetics. When she was just starting out, the famous Dr. Sam Sheppard case, which had inspired the television show and film *The Fugitive*, had just resurfaced. Sheppard's son wanted to vindicate his father. Julie was there when they exhumed the wife's body, and they found something no one in the family had known about before: a fetus in a bottle of formalin buried along with the mother. Julie attempted to extract DNA from the fetus to find out who its father was, perhaps to provide a motive for the crime. But the tissue had been in formalin too long and she couldn't extract the DNA. Still, it was an exciting event that drew her further into her profession.

Julie explains to me that she will be snipping a bit from the three places on the envelope flap that people tend to lick—the right, left, and middle. I have vivid images of Morris licking envelopes. He did it with gusto and lots of saliva. Morris was a wet kisser, a man who made a lot of mouth noises and sucking sounds. There is a picture I have from childhood of me wiping away one of his sloppy kisses. So all in all, I'm optimistic that there will be some trace of his saliva mixed in with the glue.

Julie says that they will take these snips of paper and let them sit overnight with a reagent to dissolve the organic material and the glue. Then she'll add a chemical called proteinase K, which will lyse the cells and release the DNA. As I've noted, lysis is a process that breaks the walls of the cell and dumps the contents of the cell into the reagent, resulting in a mixture of cellular debris and DNA. Introducing phenol into this liquid mixture will create a sort of three-layer parfait. The bottom layer will be the phenol, the middle will be a gunky mixture of cell parts, and floating on the top will be the DNA. The DNA can then be captured on a Microcon membrane, which is shaped like a little cup. After the DNA in the Microcon is washed with a buffer, the membrane will be inverted and the purified DNA will fall into a sterile tube.

At this point Julie will try to quantify how much DNA there is. If there is enough, she can proceed. If there isn't enough, she'll have to try again, perhaps this time trying to use saliva from the postage stamp on the envelope. When the letter was written in the 1970s, stamps were not the self-sticking kind, so the stamp, too, should contain some of Morris's saliva.

If she gets enough DNA, Julie will subject it to the same process Wayne used, the polymerase chain reaction, better known as PCR, which will cause the DNA to multiply to amounts large enough to be tested. Julie tells me that they will then look for thirteen markers—that is, thirteen places or loci in the junk DNA that are known for having lots of short tandem repeats (STRs).

A few weeks later I get a call from Julie. She's been trying to get enough DNA off the envelope to analyze it. She's gotten a bit from the flap, and a bit more from the stamp, but she doesn't have enough to do a profile yet. The problem is that the sample is old, and also that the glue and the dyes of the envelope and stamp act as inhibitors.

I'm a little disappointed, but Julie tells me that if I give her a bit more time, she might be able to use some amplification techniques to beef up the amount she has. She says that perhaps she could do a Y chromosome test, but that wouldn't necessarily tell me anything new, since I already know that Abie and Morris are brothers and share the Y chromosome. However, I tell her about the one marker mismatch between Gerald and me that the tests by Family Tree DNA had discovered.

Julie and I both realize that if she can find the mismatch in Morris's DNA on 392, this will prove without doubt that Morris is specifically linked as Gerald's father and Abie would therefore be mine. If the only two people in the Davis family who have the mismatch on 392 are Gerald and Morris, then we can also verify that the paraffin block is Morris's. Right now I know that the DNA in the paraffin block is from someone who is not my father, but I have no absolute proof that the block belongs to Morris, other than the word of the hospital.

In a few weeks I receive this e-mail from Julie:

Hello Lennard,

I wanted to give you an update. I worked with the DNA extract from the envelope flap (dated 1978) and amplified the DNA using the YSTR kit. A few loci came up but not 392. My concern about 392 is it's one of the largest fragments so we would have had to get a full pro-file in order to observe 392. It seems there is very little DNA to be had from these envelopes. If you have access to any of his clothing or a pipe or razor that might work better. Let me know if you would like a report detailing what we have done to date. Maybe we can think of something that has his DNA.

Julie

My father didn't smoke and the razor he used has been used by my son and other people. I do remember him having a comb in a hideous pink and black felt case that I sewed in second grade and gave him as a present. But I can't locate this case, although I have searched for it everywhere. So now I'm stuck with an unanswered question.

At this point, Wayne joins in this discussion. I ask Wayne if we can use the remaining slivers from the paraffin block, and Wayne thinks that we can. But Julie is worried that there may not be enough good DNA. So I call Columbia Medical Center to see if there is any more of the original paraffin block left. They tell me to write a letter, which I do.

Meanwhile, Wayne finds the DNA from Morris's previous sample, and Julie says the concentration is enough for her to work with. Wayne sends the DNA to Julie. But after some initial testing, Julie writes to me:

> With regards to the samples—I have quantified the extracts from both your sample and Morris Davis's sample. Your sample is fine and there is plenty of DNA. Morris Davis's sample is giving us some difficulty. I am trying one more procedure to quantify the DNA and if this doesn't work then I will need to speak to Dr. Grody. I will give him a call or e-mail on Monday and find out more about the sample.

Again I wait for a few weeks, and then call Julie. On the telephone, she tells me that she cannot get the DNA sample to produce enough material for further testing. We have now reached a dead end.

Trying to extract a secret from a tiny amount of dried saliva and a microns-thick shaving of biopsy tissue turns out to be a difficult business. Secrets tend to remain secrets and the occasional rays of light that we shine into the deep darkness of the past often disappear in the abyss.

Even so, my search has not been fruitless. I have been able to find out a great deal. I'm almost certain that Abie is my father, and even more certain that Morris is not. There are very few things in life one knows for sure, and most of us, even those of us without any apparent mysteries concerning our origins, have to operate on a provisional basis, using the limited knowledge we have about ourselves. I should be content to have expanded my knowledge to the point where I now know much more about my family and its origins than I did before. And I now need to accept the fact that I seem to have come to the end of what DNA testing can tell me.

TEN

Is DNA Destiny?

IN THE PROCESS OF WRITING THIS BOOK, I had some health concerns. I felt fine, but my blood tests kept coming back with some strange numbers for PSA (prostate-specific antigen). Rising PSA levels can indicate the presence of prostate cancer. My numbers were going up and down in unusual enough ways that my internist suggested I see a urologist. The urologist had me undergo a series of tests. The tests were negative, but my PSA numbers kept jumping around. This pattern could signal prostatitis, an infection of the prostate. I took some antibiotics and was retested. But the numbers didn't go down dramatically. My urologist suggested a biopsy. Another urologist suggested I wait, so now I am just doing what is called "active surveillance," a kind of educated and informed waiting and watching.

The irony will be apparent to anyone reading this book. Morris, who was not my father, died of prostate cancer, and now, even without that direct genetic legacy, I am facing it. I don't know what the future will bring. I am young enough—only fifty-eight at the moment—that there will presumably be many more years during which I might end up developing the same cancer that killed Morris and which affects 14 percent of the male population. Or I might not.

Since Morris is not my father, his genes won't influence me. But he is still almost certainly my uncle, and his proclivity toward prostate cancer could be in my genome, too, because the DNA he and I share, traveling down the Davis line, could include certain inherited mutations known to influence a man's risk of prostate cancer. Other possible genetic factors might be influential as well.

Among the mutations that increase the risk of prostate cancer are two that are generally associated with breast cancer. They involve the BRCA genes, which are genes that act as tumor suppressants. If you have one of the mutations of these genes—BRCA1 or BRCA2—your body's ability to suppress tumors is diminished. Although those particular mutations are found mainly among Ashkenazic Jews and my investigations showed that on the male side I am a Sephardic Jew, not an Ashkenazic Jew, there is still the possibility that I could have inherited them from my mother's line.

Should I continue with my DNA testing and find out if I have either the BRCA1 or BRCA2 mutation? The problem with getting this test is that if the results indicate that you have one of these mutations, there is very little you can do about it short of quite radical preventive surgery. Some women, particularly those who have seen a mother or other female relatives die of breast cancer, do have the test, and if the results reveal a mutation, some elect to have a double mastectomy in advance of any cancer. For men, however, preventive surgery involving removal of the prostate isn't advised, since the possible complications—impotence, incontinence—are ones that very few men would choose to live with if they didn't absolutely have to. Since prostate cancer tends to be slow-growing, an active surveillance program is preferred to preventive removal.

Linked to the question of what I should do with the knowledge about having or not having the BRCA1 or BRCA2 mutations is the deeper question of what an inquiry into my genetic makeup can really tell me. With so many possible permutations in the gene pool and consequently so many different strategies for dealing with the risk of disease, what is a thinking collection of DNA like myself to make of this knowledge? Even the act of trying to decide how to manage one's genetic inheritance is, on some level, being made with the brain that genetic inheritance provided. There is something profoundly paradoxical about the cognitive aspects of DNA deciding what to do about the risks caused by DNA.

I didn't embark on my quest with the goal of discovering my medical legacy. Though that is certainly a legitimate area of inquiry, my own journey was motivated more by the need to understand who I am. Now that I know, with reasonable certainty, the identity of my real father, I'm still left wondering: do your genes make you who you are, or are you something that happens in spite of your genes? Are genes like family money, where wealth can help you and poverty can hurt, but neither can absolutely determine your future? Or are genes more like instructions written into your body that can't be changed and whose outcome is inscribed with certainty? If your body has these commands written into your DNA, then how free can you be?

While many people do see DNA as destiny, the idea of a fated existence is one that has been batted about since Oedipus tried to avoid his. The language of the argument is now different, but the eternal question of free will versus fate is still unanswerable and won't be going away anytime soon. Though at first glance it may seem obvious that your genes determine your destiny, there are serious scientific as well as philosophical arguments to the contrary.

In terms of the science of genetics, one interesting line of thought that weakens the "DNA is destiny" argument concerns feedback loops. Feedback loops are interactions between an organism and its environment. On the genetic front, it is becoming increasingly clear that genes are not, as we've been told, written in stone in the Book of Life. Genes aren't fixed and unwavering. Some genes actually can respond and change depending on the environment. Feedback loops imply that a given gene can make a given amino acid but that under certain conditions that gene could be suppressed or changed by the environment.

Take, for example, mice that have been bred to have a yellow coat. Under normal circumstances, every time a yellow-coated mouse has offspring, each will have an identically colored coat. But if you feed a pregnant yellow-coated mouse a diet containing vitamin B_{12}, folic acid, choline, and betaine, the offspring will have a brown coat. When the yellow mice and brown mice were studied on the cellular level, they were all found to have the same exact genes. It was solely the change in the nutritional environment that altered the way the gene expressed itself. In other words, the gene remained the same, but the way it expressed itself changed permanently in the offspring mice, although perhaps not for future generations.

Gene expression was similarly affected when pregnant mice bred to be obese were fed soy products. The offspring mice of mothers eating soy were only a little more than half as likely to become obese as the offspring of non-soy-eating mice. Again, no changes occurred in the gene for obesity, only in the way the gene functioned.

The process by which this happened on the genetic level is called methylation. A quartet of atoms, called a methyl group, attaches itself to the gene and can suppress the function of that gene. Changes that don't involve altering the DNA sequence are called epigenetic because they happen above and beyond the "commands" set in the DNA.

Epigenetic factors have recently been discovered to play a role in the development of bats' wings. These epigenetic changes are part of what accounts for the difference between bats and mice, two species that are fairly similar genetically, having evolved from a common ancestor millions of years ago. The gene that makes a bat's bones grow into wings is exactly the same as the gene that grows the bones in a mouse's paw, with only two amino acids being different. Those two differences couldn't really be enough to create the dramatic distinction between a wing and a paw. But scientists noticed that while the bone-growth genes in bats and mice were essentially the same, the "junk" DNA near the site of the bone growth gene in the two species was slightly different. When researchers inserted this "enhancer" junk DNA from a bat into a mouse embryo, they found that the mouse's paws were much longer than normal. While the mouse's paws didn't become wings and didn't stay elongated for the lifetime of the mouse, the change lasting only a few months, the inserted junk DNA did have an epigenetic effect. That is, while the gene remained the same, it was the non-gene material that "enhanced" the effect of the gene in an epigenetic way.

It appears in these examples that DNA is definitely not destiny, or not an inalterable destiny, anyway. And if you can alter destiny, then it isn't what we call destiny.

Another, more complex, feedback loop involves the way that genes can shape or alter their own destiny. For example, the genes that led to the development of language some fifty thousand years ago, a relatively short time in human evolutionary history, created a shared symbolic system that allowed humans to change their environment dramatically. Those changes have meant that we have been able to create very different lives for ourselves as humans. Ultimately it is because of language that we have cities, cars, and the computer on which I am writing these words. We tend to think of the evolution of DNA as being confined to the mutations within the genome, but we can see that extrachromosomal forces are at work as well. Genes may have created language, but language then spurred new forms of evolution. As language became more elaborated, its use began to determine which humans would survive and which wouldn't. As the technology made possible by language developed, it, too, had an influence in natural selection. The new world created by language-using humans then selected out those who could perform well in environments involving activities predicated on complex language usage—activities such as making war.

If new groups of language-using humans were to wage war on older groups without language, the language users would have a tremendous advantage in being able to create complex war strategies and to work collaboratively to develop advanced weaponry. Agriculture and hunting are two other activities fundamental to survival in which language usage would provide a great advantage.

In our own time, group survival might be dependent on those members who are particularly good at using computers or other kinds of high-tech equipment, and groups who aren't would be at a disadvantage. In effect, our genetic survival could become dependent on human activities and functions that are no longer strictly determined by genes. As far as the future is concerned, the new environment we are even now in the process of creating might in turn be selecting for new or altered genes.

One recently discovered instance of the interaction between a human-created environment—in this case the agricultural environment—and a human DNA sequence is found in the gene governing the ability to digest milk. Scientists have discovered that the gene that creates the proteins that digest the lactose in milk is relatively new to the human race, having developed only within the past five thousand years, which is a mere drop in the evolutionary bucket. The account of this development gives us a dramatic example of how feedback loops can work. Only a small percentage of humans in the past had the gene for lactose tolerance, which gave them the ability to drink and digest unfermented dairy products. But the gene was later driven to high frequencies in the people of north-central Europe after the introduction of dairy culture to this region, because a culture that could rely on milk and milk products clearly had an evolutionary advantage in a world in which food was scarce. As the gene spread throughout northern Europe, more and more humans came to rely on and raise cows. And these people in turn affected the genetic makeup of cows, as they bred cattle to achieve greater milk production. So there was a coevolution of genes in humans and cows, and this was furthered by social and cultural developments that encouraged cattle raising, such as the introduction of money, the development of a dairy-centered cuisine, and the ability to use bacteria to produce cheese, which can be stored for future use because it lasts longer than milk and doesn't have to be consumed immediately. This remarkable feedback loop between environment and genes shows us that human activity can rewrite human genetics—and animal genetics as well.

There is also an argument floating around that evolutionary change doesn't have to come only from large genetic mutations such as a specific gene dropping out or another gene developing. Biologists such as Christopher Wills argue that very slight changes in a gene, perhaps even just the replacement of one SNP or the creation of a new STR, can alter human behavior or evolution dramatically. In fact, Wills argues, something like the development of human language might have required very little or no genetic change from the genome of our early hominid ancestors. The genes might have been there all along, requiring only a change in the environment or an alteration in some physical structure in the body to allow them to be expressed. In other words, the genes that make our brains could have been simply "waiting" for the conditions for language to arise, a new development in a feedback loop for a gene-brain system that was already there.

The next level in the story of feedback loops is the ability of humans through their technology to alter genes directly. We're already moving in that direction. We can splice new genetic sequences into the DNA of plants and animals using certain viruses as devices to carry the SNPs and STRs into the location on the DNA that we wish to change. We are hoping to be able to correct "defective" genes by supplying the "correct" sequences in mutated portions of the genome. We can now produce genetically altered crops and animals. There is substantial controversy around this kind of gene manipulation. For example, chemical giant Monsanto has created a new genetically engineered kind of corn that is capable of withstanding Monsanto's herbicide Roundup. The corn can then be grown with a no-till method using Roundup in the soil, and the corn will thrive, while all the undesirable competing weeds around it will die. Another kind of corn has been developed through genetic modification that can produce its own insecticide, obviating the need for spraying the environment. Some people fear that insects such as the monarch butterfly or honeybee may be pushed to extinction by this change in the corn's genome.

We are also moving toward genetically altering ourselves. Genetic modification of humans has been tried in the treatment of genetic diseases. So far the results have been far from good, and because some gene therapy experiments have killed rather than cured patients, this area of research has been stopped for all practical purposes.

Genetics is also altering our ideas about how to create maximally effective drugs. If we can't genetically engineer humans, then perhaps we can tailor our drugs to a person's genetic makeup rather than assuming that one drug fits all people. We are making progress toward a kind of personalized medicine in which a patient will be able to have his or her genome read in the doctor's office, and then the doctor can prescribe medications compatible with that particular patient's genetic makeup.

One field of research that is still forbidden by national and international law is tampering with the germ line of humans. The germ line is the genome specific to an animal or plant that is inherited through generations. While gene therapy aims only to change the genetic makeup of specific individuals, germ-line modification creates mutations that will be inherited by future generations. Currently, if genetic changes are made to a fetus or an adult, those changes will not show up in the sperm or eggs of that person and will not be passed down. But if any changes were to be made to an embryo, or to the sperm or egg cells themselves, those changes might be inherited by future generations. We have already changed the germ lines of animals, and though no one has yet done so with humans, increasingly there are calls for this type of intervention—particularly around the issue of inherited diseases. Thus far the possibility of making changes to the actual human genome is considered so controversial that, like the legislators who have banned it by law, most ethicists and policy makers have come out strongly against it. Yet we clearly have the technology and knowledge to try it, and it is probably only a matter of time before someone in some country does succeed at changing a germ line.

At that moment, humans will become like the gods depicted in various creation myths who are capable of creating new humans. But this story won't be a myth, it will be reality. It is now possible to imagine a future in which we can control mental and physical attributes, biochemistry, and many other aspects of what it means to be human. How Faustian a bargain this will turn out to be remains to be seen.

When we talk about the traits we've inherited from our forebears—our life expectancy probabilities, our physical resemblance to our parents, the way we have our mother's laugh or our father's gift for math, our grandfather's love of music or our grandmother's literary genius—we are all very comfortable about saying that these are "genetic." DNA has become the overarching metaphor for our twenty-first-century lives: it is the mythology that informs the language in which we tell ourselves our life stories. But it is good to remind ourselves that this is just the latest in a long line of metaphors and mythologies that humanity has used to grapple with questions of identity and destiny.

We now look down upon people in the past who talked about humors or who spoke of "bloodlines" in family histories, but we've simply substituted the new term of the moment for an outmoded one without changing much else. To call the determinants of our fate "genes" carries a ring of authority that "humors" does not. But much of our sense of destiny is tied to ideas about genetics that are vague, general, and imperfectly understood. If we understood more about the science of genetics, there would be better explanations and narratives of how our lives are—and are not—shaped by our genes.

Looking at my own life through this metaphor of genes makes me a bit philosophical. Is there any scientific rationale for my obsession with knowing whether my father was Morris or Abie? Very little, really, disease vulnerabilities aside. So in the end, while DNA has helped me identify who my father is, at this point it can't tell me much about who I am. For that, I really need to look within myself and the stories I tell myself about myself.

One of the roles I see myself playing in these stories is that of the researcher as detective who is obsessively trying to unearth the truth from the past. Side by side with that is the modern-day Oedipus searching for his father. So much of this book has been about trying to find out for sure, for absolute sure, what my origin is. But how successful have I been, really?

Some days I imagine that there is a courthouse in my head, and I'm on trial, trying to defend the conclusions I've reached against some pretty tough cross-examination. The first potential hole in my argument is that the sample I got from the hospital might not have contained Morris's DNA. A clerical error could have been made anywhere along the way, from the initial filing of the sample to the recovery of it. Then again, there could have been a mix-up in Wayne Grody's lab, even though he's extremely careful with his materials.

Another possibility is that the Y chromosome test proves nothing more than the fact that I am a Davis—like Morris and Abie, and like Gerald, Leslie, and Frank. And if Gerald's one-marker difference from me occurred in his own generation, rather than in

Morris's, it wouldn't be able to tell me anything about whether or not I was Morris's son.

In the end, I just have Abie's assertion to me that fateful day, Leslie's eventual confirmation that his father had told him the same thing, and some genetic testing that is not inconsistent with that conclusion, although not enough to confirm it absolutely. But since Abie was not necessarily to be trusted, his testimony to both of us could be called into question.

If I was subjected to this kind of cross-examination, I could certainly defend myself. I might point out that the hospital had no trouble finding the sample and it checked out against Morris's name, address, and social security number. Wayne's office was meticulous about its protocols. His office did produce a definitive result showing that Morris wasn't my father. My Y chromosome tests did confirm that I was a Davis and that I matched Abie's son Leslie exactly and also my second cousin Frank, while I was one marker off from Gerald. All in all, I am fairly certain that Abie's story, corroborated by Leslie and by my own personal memories of family life and lore, is true. And ultimately I have to feel that while absolute certainty is almost never possible, the preponderance of evidence does point to my being Abie's biological son.

William Wordsworth wrote, "The Child is the father of the Man." I think he meant that what happens to the child, the child's world and experiences, gives birth to the adult he or she later becomes. In that sense, this story involves my trying to midwife the child who then gave birth to the adult me. In delving into not only my childhood but also the genes that have made me, I've both become newly born and grown up anew.

One place that I have rediscovered this child who fathered me is in my dreams. I mentioned earlier that I have a recurring dream that involves my apparently having committed a murder in the past and buried a body beneath the cellar floor. In the dream I can't remember the details of the murder, or even if I really did it, but I definitely buried a body and I am fairly certain that the floor of the basement still contains the body or bodies. I wake up, always con-fused for a few minutes as I regain consciousness about whether or not I did commit a murder in reality, and it always takes me a while to realize that I am innocent.

In a recent version of this dream my friend Ralph, who is an economist, is trying to find out about the murder. He's persistent and is plumbing the Internet for information. I feel the web of sus-picion drawing tighter. Ralph won't be deterred, and now he's in the basement sweeping the dirt floor with a broom. A filing cabinet or metal container is being unearthed. I feel certain that the body will be discovered and I'll be sent to jail. Ralph digs up the box and opens it. It's completely empty, without any trace of a body or any body parts or spoor. This new version of the dream is different from all my previous ones. This is the first time the dream shows some-thing actually being dug up. And it is not a body, merely an empty file box. The way I interpret this is that the file box has replaced the body, and the file box could represent my notes for this book, or my laboratory file.

I'm increasingly feeling that this dream is about my own re-birth. The body symbolizes someone—perhaps Abie, Morris, Eva, or even me—whom I had to kill to become me now. There is a sense that my being in the world is premised on some primal guilt, some major forgetting, that had to happen for me to be born. And now, perhaps as a result of finding out what I have, of finding the child who is the father to the man, the corpse is gone. There doesn't have to be a body or some primal repression for me to be myself. Am I free from the curse of Delphi? Perhaps I've finally learned that I am not guilty of any crime. There's nothing in the box.

ELEVEN

Endings and Beginnings

WHEN I TELL PEOPLE MY STORY, they always ask how I feel about my discovering that Abie is my father. At this point in my life I have to say that I feel pretty good. I'm relieved that I'm not Morris's son. Morris was too complicated a man and his relations with me too fraught for me to be content with him as a father. I'm happy to know the truth of my paternity and to reconcile all the odd feelings I had as a child through a narrative that now makes sense of those feelings.

And what about Abie?

I had another dream recently: Abie and I are walking along the street. He has asked me to go to dinner with him. He looks a bit fat, but is wearing a suit and tie and is quite dapper. I make excuses about how busy I am, and clearly don't want to go. He's upset and then trips and falls down into the gutter, as if he's weakened or ill. I suddenly feel sorry for him and say, "Of course I'll have dinner with you." I wake up and find myself crying in the middle of the night.

Who is Abie? I never really knew him, so he's just a construct of

Abie and me at my bar mitzvah

memories carried over from the mind of a small child to an adult who is still in thrall to that childhood. Abie is all that is bad, immoral, and untrustworthy. He's a loser—unclean, tardy, sexual, rambunctious, and rebellious. He is the id and the monster, the half-human man with a large cleft in his head, a cross between a kind of Frankenstein and a freeloading houseguest. You'd never have dinner with him if you had a choice.

In reality, what was he? His son, Leslie, is deeply alienated from him, so I can't claim he was a good father. On the other hand, his perceived sexual looseness may have been just that—a perception, and a misconception at that. It's possible that my sense of Abie's sexuality was so exaggerated because that was the elephant in the room every time Abie came around—the unspoken fact that it was

Abie's sperm that impregnated my mother. After Abie's wife died, he was a single man in New York, and he dated a string of women. Perhaps from my father's Victorian/Edwardian perspective, this made Abie look sleazy. But if that is the case, there are many sleazy men in New York. That he didn't find a wife right away may have been a sign that he couldn't commit or didn't want to commit. Or it may have been that he couldn't find someone he liked. In fact, I remember that my parents talked about setting him up with my second-grade teacher, Miss Berg, a large, homely woman with paisley-shaped eyeglasses who looked like she stepped out of a Gary Larson cartoon. No wonder he kept looking! He eventually, years later, lived with and married a woman from Thailand. He had met her on a trip there, and though the relationship turned out badly, I do know that this ex-wife was one of the few people who came to his funeral, long after they had divorced.

Abie, like Morris, was an avid athlete. His sport was soccer, and he was very good at it. So why didn't I remember him as athletic? I know that his son, Leslie, still regards his father's athleticism and persistence at the game as one of his only redeeming attributes. My view of my uncle was probably colored by the fact that my father didn't give full credit to Abie as a sportsman. Because Abie didn't do track and field, the sports Morris participated in, and Morris was not interested in soccer, he seems simply to have dismissed Abie's achievements. He instilled in my mind that it was he who was the true athlete, while Abie was just a dabbler, a loafer, a ne'er-do-well.

I realize that I've succeeded, until recently, in banishing Abie from my world, just as my parents wanted. He was banned from the honored place of a father, and also, because of the constant admonitions of my parents, not allowed to be someone I might have loved as an uncle or looked to as a mentor. Now the dream seems to be telling me that the Abie in me needs to be known, seen, and dined with. Because the actual Abie is dead, however, I'll never have a chance to reconcile with him through these means. But I can still try to see the ways in which Abie lives on in me. He might well represent that part of me that is the rebel. My father always had a rigid moral sense of right and wrong, as did my mother. I walk around with the guilt of knowing that my stan- dards of behavior don't always fall into such neat categories. I try to behave in a manner of which my parents would have approved, but sometimes I don't, and sometimes I think the categories them- selves are too inflexible. But there were no exceptions in my par- ents' world. Moralists don't give out free passes or days off.

Abie, then, may represent the wayward part of me, the part that might fall in the gutter, or put more generously, that aspect of me that doesn't need to judge, that sees what I do and accepts myself as simply human—errant, wayward, uncertain, following desires as old as the human race. I don't have to solve the problem of right and wrong; I just have to accept that both exist and that I can't always be sure which is which. This doesn't mean I can't live an ethical life; it just means I have to come up with my own criteria, which don't have to derive from my father's quasi-biblical laws. Abie is my ticket out of the world of absolute shoulds and musts. Moses (Morris's Hebrew name) offers to lead me to the Promised Land, but only if I don't dance before the golden calf. Abie, Avram, the old progeni- tor, already lives there, perhaps foolish, perhaps fooled, but he is in his tent waiting for me to come and join the revelries.

Since it's too late for me to join Abie in any literal sense, however, I remind myself that his son, now my half brother, Leslie, or Les, as he prefers to be called, is very much alive. I've contacted him by phone a number of times in this quest of mine, we've written back and forth on e-mail, and he very generously complied with my request to have genetic testing done on him. But I haven't seen him since Abie's funeral more than twenty years ago. Now I feel that I should go visit him—after all, he's my brother.

I've been hesitant to do so because although Les has been very sweet to me all along, and we now sign our e-mails "love" and "your brother," I still feel the visceral revulsion toward Abie that my parents instilled in me. As much as I've mentally tried to rehabilitate Abie, I can't stop seeing him as that somewhat scary and distasteful uncle of my youth. And Les is no doubt a lovely man, but he plays the role of the son of the unsavory father in the proscenium of my archaic emotional theater.

Les lives an hour's drive from me on Long Island, near JFK airport. I call him up and ask him if I can visit. He is agreeable, but he's had a bad fall, as a result of a troubling and still undiagnosed illness, and since his face is badly bruised and he's still sometimes very dizzy, this week seems out.

Finally, the following week, we are able to set a date. Les suggests we meet at a diner near him.

I drive out to Cedarhurst, Long Island, on a drizzly October day. The ride to JFK airport is never a particularly nice one, but it seems grimmer than usual on this trip. As I skirt the perimeter of the massive airport, I feel depressed, as if I were in some kind of wasteland of the soul. That vision is reinforced as I recall that my parents are buried nearby, under the glide path to the airport. I went there in the early days after their deaths, to stand by the increasingly overgrown graves in the huge Jewish cemetery where they lie. My graveside reveries always seemed to be accompanied by the grinding whine of a 747 as it passed overhead. The din was a constant mechanical dirge amidst the silence of the departed. Of course, living or dead, my parents were deaf to it all. Now I am driving by them, by the secret they took with them to their graves, as I cruise on the highway to see Les. Everything seems to be coming together.

The Sherwood Diner is a robust memorial to fifty years of Jewish overeating. It stands in a strip mall beside a busy thoroughfare of trucks and automobiles, a polished metal and opaque-green glass extravaganza. Its theme—Sherwood Forest and Robin Hood—seems inexplicable in this highway setting. What do piles of corned beef and lox have in common with Maid Marian and Friar Tuck? Yet, despite the British-Jewish theme, or because of it, the place feels incredibly familiar to me and provides a portal back to my childhood. I arrive early, and so have a chance to sit in a booth by a window looking onto a parking lot. Garish Halloween decorations hang from the acoustic tile ceiling. Behind me is a large aquarium in which swim slow-moving distant relations of the whitefish appetizer and nova lox that are specialties of the diner. But there's one speedy catfish doing frenetic laps as if to avoid the fate of his finny cousins on the platters. Older couples sit together stuffing down large plates of roasted chicken or baked salmon. Younger people wolf hamburgers and fries.

The waitress, a pleasant woman whose name tag identifies her as Angela, serves me a platter of pickles and marinated cabbage within milliseconds of my sitting down. A basket filled with challah bread and warm brioches arrives shortly thereafter. My discomfort and fears flee as I taste the various madeleines of my kosher childhood. The Sherwood Diner could be a perfect location for anyone who wanted to make a movie of my early life.

Within minutes Les arrives, accompanied by his wife, Marlene. We haven't seen each other for over twenty years, but I recognize Les instantly. He looks so much like Abie.

The years have been hard on Les. He's pale and wobbly on his feet. Though still overweight, he tells me he's lost forty pounds in the last few months—his shirt looks large and his belt a bit long now. His weight gain was probably related to the diabetes that he also shares with Abie. His wife, too, has had health problems. She tells me as she sits down that chemotherapy has made her brain a bit addled, and if I notice any misuse of words or lack of clarity, I should chalk it up to the ravages of the chemicals. In fact, I don't notice any such thing.

Les is four years older than I am, an age gap that now seems insignificant, although when we were children I always saw him as being much older than I. His face, which has aged a lot, is covered with moles, and he has a fatty lump on his forehead. I mention that because Morris had the same type of lump for many years until it was surgically removed.

Between the pickles and the challah and the familiar sight of that lump, I now feel completely at home. Les, despite his physical problems, is bright and has a wonderful sense of humor. There is a smile on his face and a twinkle in his eye that shine through a film of sadness. Les has been an advertising copywriter and publicist all these years, putting his humor and intelligence to good use. And he's won prizes for his endeavors. Engaging as he is, and as much as I immediately warm to him, I don't feel instantly as if this is my brother. In fact, I can't see any resemblance to me, except in the eyes, while Les's resemblance to Abie is very strong. A part of me feels that I'm here to reexperience Abie, to see in this son the sides of him I didn't know. It's as if the DNA that we've been trying to find is suddenly all there before me, coalesced into this familiar face.

I ask Les to tell me what he liked about Abie.

"Well, he was very intelligent. He loved science and was endlessly interested in discovering the natural world, technology, how things worked."

This is news to me, and I feel a leaping sense of connection in my soul. I don't need Dr. Sichell. Abie was a natural intellectual in his own right.

"And he loved soccer, was a very good athlete."

Les tells me the story again of how Abie would play five or six games on a Saturday, after working all week, and only be able to do that by using pseudonyms, since the soccer regulations forbade playing multiple games. It turns out that Abie was quite fond of pseudonyms. He used to open bank accounts using our grandmother's maiden name—Moskowitz. And even his own full name included a pseudonym, as Les explains when he tells me the story about how Abie got his scar.

"When Abie was quite young, his sister Janie threw a pair of scissors at him. You know, the very large kind of shears that our grandmother used for cutting the fabric. The scissors stuck in Abie's skull and fractured the bone. He was rushed to the hospital, but, you know, back then they didn't do brain surgery, and there was a lot of damage."

Les tells me that our grandparents called in a Hasidic Jew to do an exorcism on Abie, which involved changing his name from Abraham to Abraham Aaron. The orthodox believe that if you change your name, you can fool the Angel of Death into thinking you are someone else when he comes to fetch you, and then he'll leave. I remember that this was the very same maneuver that Abie used when Morris nearly died of acute renal failure, and both name changes seem to have saved the lives of the potential victims.

As Les talks, I start seeing signs everywhere. Abie's pseudonyms are some kind of a sign of the elusiveness of his character, which is hard to see below the surface. The fish in the aquarium behind me, darting back and forth through the murk, are another sign, reminding me that I can only see Abie through a glass darkly.

Continuing his reminiscences, Les tells me that Abie was very protective of Morris when he was in the hospital. I remember that Abie did a lot of research and was concerned that Morris wasn't getting the best care. At the time I thought he was being a bit paranoid, but looking back on it now, he was probably right.

We talk a bit more and then order our food. Everyone starts out with matzoh ball soup, one of the specialties of the Sherwood Diner, no doubt the soup of choice for Robin and his merry band. The soup arrives, a giant dumpling wedged in a small cup with the broth a barely perceptible eddy around the great white ball. This is clearly the Moby Dick of matzoh balls. One taste and I realize that I've speared with my spoon the platonic ideal of Jewish cuisine. Seeing Les and Marlene eating the soup, I am back in the Bronx, a small boy at the metal-topped kitchen table with no idea that my weird uncle is actually my father, feeling anchored in the childhood security of a life that seems to be as solid and real as a side of pastrami.

As we eat, Les tells me that at one point Abie owned his own business—a leather store that made novelty items, located at 1 Union Square in Manhattan. This is a complete shock to me. When I later went to that address to check it out, I found a distinguished-looking, late-nineteenth-century Richardsonian-style building facing what is now the very trendy Union Square Park. The storefront has large windows that open onto a grand sales space. As I conjure up a vision of my uncle as the proprietor of this space, I try to reconcile it with the image of the man my father always described as a slacker and a loser. Morris, who never became anything more than a day laborer in a factory, managed to cast his brother as a failure. Yet it was Abie who was the owner of a business and Morris who didn't amount to much beyond his athletics. How did I not know this?

Les dutifully tells me about the upside of Abie, but you can see that he really wants to talk about the downside. And the downward slope was steep and deadly.

"He was a sadist," Les says, and you can see enough hurt in the eyes of this sixty-two-year-old man to let you know that he still feels the pain of his youth. "He beat me with a belt. He always raised welts, but sometimes so bad that I bled. He hit my mother, and actually once broke her dentures. She left him several times, once for a year. He was psychologically cruel. He'd insult me and make me feel bad about everything I did. He once hit me while we were driving because he asked me directions and I pointed the wrong way. He made me write 'I will respect my father' so many times that my hand swelled up. After my mother died when I was eleven, he made me do the cooking, the cleaning, the shopping."

Although Morris, too, was sometimes cruel, he's beginning to look saintly and restrained compared with Abie. But neither of them could control their tempers very well. And apparently neither could their sister Janie, the one with the good throwing arm and the scissors.

"He knew he was out of control," Les says. "Once when he hit me—I was young, eleven or twelve, but I had a good vocabulary—I said to him, 'You're not a good father, you're a sadist!' And he actually cried. Right there he sat down after hitting me and just sobbed."

I tell Les that my parents warned me against being like Abie.

"What did they warn you against?"

"Being late, reading in bed, reading on the toilet, staying in bed in the morning and wearing my pajamas. Something about being sexually questionable."

Les laughs. "If those were his biggest faults, it would have been fine." He mentions that he once found a cache of pornography his father had. I ask him if he felt uncomfortable with his father's dating women. He said he didn't, but mentioned that his father was addicted to gambling and perhaps to sex. Yet it's odd that Morris protected me from the worst aspect of Abie, his sadism, and just focused on the relatively minor sins.

When Les's mother, Sally, died, her family wanted to adopt him, but Abie wouldn't allow it. Abie must have feared, Les thinks, that they would have turned his son against him. The irony, of course, is that Abie turned his son against him without any outside help. I wonder why my family didn't want to adopt Les. If he had come to live with us, I could have had a brother much closer to my own age than Gerald. Why didn't the families spend more time together, given that we lived just a few blocks apart?

"Maybe Morris didn't want to be reminded," Les speculates. I think he's right. It wasn't that the brothers didn't like each other. Later in life, when they were both widowed, they traveled to England together, shared a hotel room, and had good stories to tell about the trip. But Les describes the way they typically interacted with each other. They would argue, both of them speaking sign language, which Abie had learned, until Morris, wanting to put an end to the argument, would cover his eyes so that he would no longer be able to see Abie's side of the conversation. Then Abie would stamp his feet on the floor to try to make Morris pay attention. What an apt image for the whole secret! Morris, refusing to acknowledge Abie's active involvement in his life, covers his eyes and tries to shut Abie out.

Les tells me some more stories about the family. One he remembers captures the rivalry among the Davis men. Morris was boast-

Morris and Sol

ing to his father and his brother about his accomplishments as a race-walker. Perhaps in frustration with his braggadocio, Sol and Abie bet him that they could walk as fast as he could, and the three of them entered a walking race. Sol was so determined to prevail that he vowed to give up smoking and start training again, to get himself into shape. They all did very well, and Sol even ended up beating his champion son because he'd been given quite a handicap for his age. Much gloating ensued.

Les tells me that before his illness, he himself could lift very heavy weights. Now he's bragging, too. The family rivalries seem to live on. He mentions one time when he was dared by a friend to prove his strength. In a moment not unlike the one with Sol, Abie, and Morris, Les and the friend went off to the gym, where Les proceeded to press 750 pounds with his legs. Whether the poundage is accurate, there is no doubt that Les could push a lot of weight with his lower body. Now much debilitated, Les takes obvious pleasure in his former prowess.

Telling this story, he notes that the men in the Davis family all had the trait of stubbornness—with both its positive and negative aspects. The positive aspect is determination, and the negative is sheer bullheadedness. Les tells me about the day when Sol, who was living in Los Angeles at the time, went fishing and hooked a shark on his line. Solomon was short but powerful and the shark was big and powerful. Onlookers were telling him to cut the line but Sol wasn't about to give up the shark. Even after the shark had lacerated his hand, Sol would not abandon the struggle. Looking like the old man of Hemingway's story, he finally landed the beast. When he took the shark to Sea World, where he worked, he got $100 for it, but his medical treatment cost much more. I think about my father's resolution when he engaged in race-walking, remembering that his favorite motto was "Never say die!" It was probably that same kind of persistence that led him to ask Abie to donate his sperm so that he and my mother could at last realize their dream of having another child.

And then I think about how it's also the same kind of determination—or is it just stubbornness?—that has brought me to this diner, that has made me stick to this fool's errand of trying to find out who my father is.

The manic catfish continues to swim frantically from side to side of the small aquarium behind me, as if setting an example or a counterexample. I look across the table at my cousin, now half

Les and me

brother. I think about my dead fathers. And suddenly I'm filled with a kind of gratitude. I'm grateful to have made it here, to be sitting down to dinner with someone with whom I would probably never have been in the same room until one of our funerals. I'm grateful for the bounteous bagel and lox "all the way." Life suddenly seems full and rich. It's not that I feel that I have much in common with Les—I don't—but I do suddenly feel close to him as the living reminder of all the human drama that went into the making of me.

We move on to dessert. Angela, the waitress, recommends strawberry shortcake, which was my childhood favorite along with charlotte russe. It was my required cake for any birthday, and suddenly today feels like a birthday. Angela has overheard some of the conversation and she joins in. She tries to see a resemblance between Les and me, and decides that it's all in the eyes. That's also what I thought.

Angela's got a few family stories of her own, and she also has been trying to research her family origins, back in Sicily. I think how desperately humans want to know where they come from, who their people are, what the deep story is behind the superficial fact of having been born. Angela's tried to trace her family's history in Sicily, but she hasn't gotten very far. She needs to find an expert genealogist to help her, but she says that is too expensive. Angela is a working woman, with limited time and resources, and she doesn't have the spare cash to pay people to do some of the research, to track down the necessary documents. She's debating whether the knowledge is worth the cost. I tell her it's worth it, and I'm feeling that it really is.

As we sit eating the shortcake, I can't shake the feeling that I've come home in some way. It's a strange way, out here in a diner in Cedarhurst with Les and his wife. It doesn't make too much sense, but it feels right. Morris isn't my father, and Abie isn't the father I want. But Abie had some good traits—intelligence, inquisitiveness, ability with science, sports acumen, entrepreneurship, even protective love for Morris. He wasn't all bad, and I'd like to think that I've acquired the good without too much of the bad. I feel kind of lucky, like someone who's been given the opportunity to sift through a yard sale before anyone else arrives. I didn't get to pick the qualities of my fathers, but fate seems to have made a pretty good selection for me. And unlike the shadow figure of Oedipus, who has dogged my story, I'm not fated to find that I have identified the wrong man as my father; rather, I have reached this resolution, late in the game, that given the genetic threads that run through a family, both of my fathers have been in some way the "right man"—helping me become my own man.

When it comes time to say goodbye, Les stands up on his unstable legs. We're both a little awkward. I hug Les, and a strange thing happens to me. I don't want to stop hugging him. Is there some family pheromone in common that triggers this response in me? Am I hanging on so tightly because I now understand he's part of me, a part I am just beginning to reconnect with, and I know that when the hug stops, the intensity of the connection will be diminished? Some very visceral part of myself is connecting to this man in a simple and human way. I hang on for a few seconds too long. Les starts to pull back, and the moment is over. I hope Les perceives my embrace as a sign of affection and not lunacy. Then we wave goodbye and separate into the frank ugliness of the suburban strip mall. The merry band disperses from Sherwood, having robbed from the dead and given to the living.

When I come back home, I try to listen to the digital device I've bought to record the event. I've paid a couple of hundred bucks for a top-of-the-line product that I can turn directly into text on my computer. But there's nothing on it. Its electronic sophistication is obviously too high for my lower-level technological know-how. So, the two hours of conversation are now only a trace in my brain. This is somehow fitting. I've tried to recover so much from a past that left so few records. I've managed to extract traces of DNA, bits of the dead passed down from lost progenitors. I've had to remember fragments from the past, piece together different testimonies and recollections, talk to a lot of people, and the final result—what's in my head, what's in my heart, and what I've written down—is what will last.

Have I arrived at truth? Do I have knowledge? The ancient Greeks felt that knowledge, true knowledge, was the equivalent of knowing that life is tragic. Wisdom is a kind of resigned grief. After all is said and done, I think I have reached a kind of knowing resignation. I feel certain that my father is Abie. But I also feel, rather than grief, a kind of joy—the pleasure that comes from having made the attempt to know. I am the kind of person who deeply believes that the unexamined life is not worth living, but I am also aware that the overexamined life might not be worth living, either. So for me the examination has come to a resting point—a point of stasis. My obsession has been satisfied, which means it is not an obsession anymore.

I have an old bottle of champagne I've been saving for the right moment. After coming home from the Sherwood Diner, I decide to pop the cork. Sitting alone in my study, I toast them all—Morris, Eva, Abie, Solomon. Their story has been, if not completely revealed, at least brought to light. I toast the idea that it is better to know than not to know. I toast my brothers, Gerald and Les. I toast the mysterious mix of genes that make me who I am and whose little inconsistencies allow me and others to determine the truth about the past from the nucleic acids of the present.

I put my lips to the rim of the flute and feel the effervescence of the aged wine brought to life by the pop of the cork. I taste the light spume and the darker undertones of the champagne, and feel the deep pleasure of being alive, having been brought into the sparkle of this world by the serendipity of circumstance and the determined actions of a few whose goal was to bring me to this very moment where I might, in fact, drink to the lees from this complex and full brew of life.

ACKNOWLEDGMENTS

I want to thank all the principals in this book for their time and effort, particularly my family members, who were generous with me during all the emotional and factual upheavals that went along with the twists and turns of my personal story. I also offer my appreciation to my friends and loved ones who do not appear in the book but who are an integral part of it by virtue of their support and connection with me.

A substantial thank-you to Dr. Wayne Grody of the UCLA Medical Center, who provided his time, staff, and energy in helping me to decode my and my relatives' DNA and sort through the implications of what we found. Had he not casually offered to help me, then a virtual stranger to him, I doubt this book would have been written.

Thanks to my agent, Elisabeth Weed, who with humor and warmth provided unlimited help and support, and without whom this book definitely would never have been published. Also thanks to Melissa Flashman at Trident Media, who helped me formulate the early form and structure of this book. My appreciation also goes to Walter Benn Michaels for introducing me to Melissa, who in turn introduced me to Elisabeth Weed.

When I worked with him on the episode of *This American Life* where my story first appeared in public, Ira Glass used his organizational savvy to help me put the story in some kind of order and to help me understand the arc of my narrative. Thanks, too, to the staff of that wonderful radio show, including Julie Snyder, Wendy Dorr, Jane Feltes, Diane Cook, and many other technicians and interns.

Finally, thanks to my editor, Beth Rashbaum, for her faith in this project. Her comprehensive editorial skills turned this from a good-enough book into a much better book, and in the process she helped me see how to sharpen my writing and my rhetorical logic.

ABOUT THE AUTHOR

LENNARD J. DAVIS is a professor of English, Disability Studies, and Medical Education at the University of Illinois at Chicago. He divides his time between Chicago and New York.